Text Classics

ETHEL FLORENCE LINDESAY RICHARDSON was born in Melbourne in 1870. When she was nine her father died after being admitted to Melbourne's Kew mental asylum. His illness and suffering had a huge impact on his family.

After his death, Richardson's mother took her children to Maldon, where she worked as the postmistress.

Richardson was sent to board at Presbyterian Ladies' College in 1883—an experience that provided material for her novel, *The Getting of Wisdom*. At school she developed into a talented pianist and tennis player.

In 1888, she travelled to Europe with her mother and studied at the Leipzig Conservatorium, where she met John George Robertson, a Scottish expert in German literature. The pair married and settled in London. She published her first novel, *Maurice Guest*, in 1908, under the pen name Henry Handel Richardson, which she used for all of her books.

Richardson made her only journey back to Australia in 1912 to complete her research for the trilogy that would become *The Fortunes of Richard Mahony*. Her final novel, *The Young Cosima*, appeared in 1939. Henry Handel Richardson died in Sussex in 1946. Her unfinished memoir, *Myself When Young*, was published posthumously in 1948.

BRENDA NIALL is one of Australia's foremost biographers. Her acclaimed biography *Mannix* won the 2016 Australian Literature Society's Gold Medal for Literature and the National Biography Award. In 2004 she was awarded the Order of Australia for 'services to Australian literature, as an academic, biographer and literary critic'.

ALSO BY HENRY HANDEL RICHARDSON

Maurice Guest
The Getting of Wisdom
The Fortunes of Richard Mahony
The Young Cosima
Two Studies
The End of a Childhood
The Adventures of Cuffy Mahony

Myself When Young
Henry Handel Richardson

Text Publishing Melbourne Australia

textclassics.com.au
textpublishing.com.au

The Text Publishing Company
Swann House
22 William Street
Melbourne Victoria 3000
Australia

First published by William Heinemann 1948.

This edition published by The Text Publishing Company 2019.

Cover design by W. H. Chong.
Cover art: Rupert Bunny, *The yellow scarf, portrait of Henry Handel Richardson*, National Library of Australia.
Page design by Text.
Typeset by Midland Typesetting.

Printed in Australia by Griffin Press, part of Ovato, an Accredited ISO AS/NZS 14001:2004 Environmental Management System printer.

ISBN: 9781925773958 (paperback)
ISBN: 978195774719 (ebook)

A catalogue record for this book is available from the National Library of Australia.

CONTENTS

No Bouquets,
No Touching Up
by Brenda Niall

SOME MEMOIRS are written in tranquil mood and quiet spaces. Not this one. When Henry Handel Richardson sat down at her desk in September 1942 to contemplate her younger self, the sound of German bombing raids made writing almost impossible. Yet she found the task a welcome escape from the turbulent present. A novel in progress and a short story were put aside. *Myself When Young* was her last book. Although she did not live to complete it, her memoir opens a door to her past that she had kept firmly closed during her life as a writer.

After her husband's death in 1933, Richardson had moved from London to Sussex. Her house, Green Ridges, chosen for its seclusion and its spectacular views of sea and coastal cliffs, happened to be in the flight path of German bombers bound for London and other strategic targets. Night after night her house shook: the windows rattled and once or twice their glass shattered. In interludes of quietness Richardson began to write her reminiscences.

Richardson had always resisted questions about her younger self. Her identity as Australian-born Ethel Florence Lindesay Richardson, wife of London-based scholar John George Robertson, was concealed from the literary world under the pseudonym Henry Handel Richardson. 'Mrs Robertson did not write my books', she insisted.

The male pseudonym was partly a game she wanted to play. Would anyone suspect that her first novel, *Maurice Guest* (1908), was a woman's work? She won that round; no one guessed that this powerful study of obsessive love, set among music students in Leipzig, had been written by a woman, let alone a young Australian newcomer to Europe. And although her next novel, *The Getting of Wisdom* (1910), came very close to her own experience at Melbourne boarding school Presbyterian Ladies' College, the expatriate author's identity remained a secret. The few friends who knew the truth respected Richardson's fiercely maintained privacy. Those who were shocked by this candid account of the author's schooling wanted her identity kept quiet. But the author's hidden self couldn't withstand the spectacular success, in 1929, of *Ultima Thule*, the final volume of the trilogy *The Fortunes of Richard Mahony*. The first two volumes, *Australia Felix* (1917) and *The Way Home* (1924), had been disappointingly received; and without a subsidy from her husband, *Ultima Thule* might not have come to light. When it eventually appeared, critics compared its tragic vision with the greatest European novels, especially those of Dostoevsky.

Even when she became a celebrity, with huge sales in the United States, Richardson revealed very little about herself. Reporters had to work with snippets, and they made conjectures that amused and annoyed the author. Having her name given as 'Henrietta' was a persistent irritant; her birth name of Ethel Florence Lindesay Richardson was equally unacceptable.

Being Henry was essential to Richardson's sense of self. It was also her defence. She insisted that she needed a mask to hide behind, or a 'straw man' to take her place against attack. With half a lifetime of being called Henry, even by her husband, it would be hard to unmask for the public in a memoir. Why then, did she write *Myself When Young*? She had already confronted the ghosts of her past and turned them to fiction. Richard and Mary, in the Mahony trilogy are not her parents, Walter and Mary Richardson; nor is Laura in *The Getting of Wisdom* the author's self. Yet the novels in which they appear could not have been written without much searching and questioning of herself, her family and the events that had shaped her. Having scrutinised her memories and turned them, often painfully, into great art, hadn't she done enough?

One reason was clear. The fame she had won with *Ultima Thule* meant that, at some time, someone would write her biography. She would be an elusive subject for an American or English biographer. For an Australian, the task might seem easier. The obvious potential biographer was Nettie Palmer, Australia's most influential literary critic of the time. Henry respected Nettie's intelligence and admired her dedication. The two women had much in common. They had been to the same school in Melbourne; they had both studied in Germany; they were both formidable intellectuals. Fifteen years younger than Henry, Nettie was close enough to understand her subject and distant enough to judge.

Yet there was a catch. Nettie had two passions: her novelist husband, Vance Palmer, and her dedication to the advancement of Australian literature. Henry thought Vance's novels were boring and stodgy, and she did not want her own work to be defined by its Australian-ness. And there were some old grievances. Before the immense success of *Ultima Thule*, Nettie had written patronisingly about the 'faded charm' of the second volume of the Mahony trilogy. She had missed the point of *The Getting of Wisdom*, dismissing it as a conventional school story rather than a portrait of an artist in the making. She had no sense of humour, Henry concluded. 'Nettie Palmer! What on earth could *she* know of my younger self?' she wrote after Nettie had approached her about a biography.[1] The only way to ward off Nettie—and presumably others—was to write her own story.

'When I *do* take pen in hand to write about myself & my work I shall always speak the blunt truth', Henry wrote in 1941. 'I can't afford to go about nursing other people's feelings.'[2]

So she began to write *Myself When Young*. The first part was easy. I am 'prancing forward with the Reminiscences', she wrote in a letter to a friend. She found it intriguing to analyse the 'particular small child that was me.'[3] Her idea of biography was 'absolute truthfulness: no bouquets, no touching up'.[4] That had to be her approach to her own history.

Although there are lapses from the 'absolute truth', so far as anyone can know it, *Myself When Young* reconstructs her past without self-serving evasions. She characterises herself as a difficult child, jealous of her pretty younger sister, Lilian, not much liked at school, and irritable with her mother, whose strength and generosity she nevertheless acknowledges.

The dominant fact of her early life was her father's physical and mental breakdown. Intellectually gifted, at first successful as a medical practitioner and for a time a lucky investor in Victoria's golden age, Walter Richardson's illness left his family unprovided for. Henry remembered him as a 'poor broken creature' whose public episodes of dementia were an embarrassment to her nine-year-old self. When he was declared insane, and confined in the public mental asylum in Melbourne, it was more than his wife could bear. She petitioned for his release and brought him home to die. For his daughter, his death came as a relief; it was many years before she read his letters and understood his suffering.

Mary Richardson worked as a postmistress in Victorian country towns so as to educate her two daughters: Ethel (then known as Ettie) and Lilian. Ettie and Lil were musically gifted. When the family fortunes improved, Mary Richardson took them to Leipzig, so that Ettie could train as a concert pianist. But that dream collapsed. As told in *Myself When Young,* Ettie could not bear the scrutiny of an audience's gaze, but it also seems likely that, as biographers suggest, she lacked the exceptional quality that makes a concert pianist.

The final section of Richardson's memoir traced a happy time as a music student in Leipzig, where she met her future husband. John George Robertson, a scholarly Scot, became mentor and friend as well as devoted husband to the gifted, emotionally fragile Richardson. The relief with which she found herself 'safely and soundly married' resounds on the last pages of *Myself When Young.*

From September 1942 until her death in March 1946, Richardson worked on her memoirs. She persisted in spite of the threats and distractions of war, blackouts, rationing of food and petrol, recurrent ill health, as well as loneliness and the knowledge that all her books were out of print and likely to be forgotten. Advanced colon cancer was diagnosed in November 1944, and emergency surgery gave only a short respite. She returned to her memoirs, often in acute pain, writing a little at a time, stoically uncomplaining.

Richardson was able to die at home because of the loving care and companionship of Olga Roncoroni, a young amateur pianist, for whose acute, disabling anxiety Henry had taken immense trouble to arrange treatment. Olga came to the Richardson household in distress and stayed for many years to become its strength. Without Olga, 'a jewel of a girl', as Richardson described her, the memoir would never have been written. It closes with Olga's postscript recording the courage with which Henry Handel Richardson met her death at the age of seventy-six, leaving the memoir unfinished yet unforgettable in its self-awareness, its wry comedy and its candid recall of her Australian childhood.

1 HHR to Mary Kernot, 29 January 1943, in Clive Probyn and Bruce Steele (eds), *Henry Handel Richardson: The Letters*, Miegunyah Press, Melbourne, 2000.
2 HHR to Mary Kernot, 10 June 1941, *Letters.*
3 HHR to Oliver Stonor, 19 November 1942, *Letters.*
4 HHR to Mary Kernot, 10 June 1941, *Letters.*

Myself When Young

PART I

I

It has never been my way to say much about my private life. Rightly or wrongly, I believed this only concerned myself. And I trusted to my husband to supply, on my death, any further information that might be asked for. Now that he is gone, however, there is no one to take his place, and so I propose to jot down a few facts about myself, and memories of my childhood, which may possibly be of interest to some who have read my books.

First to touch, very briefly, on my parents. My father, Walter Lindesay Richardson, was a native of Dublin, the descendant of two Irish families, the Lindesays and the Richardsons, who had inter-married in the eighteenth century. He was the youngest child of my grandfather's second marriage—at the age of seventy-two to a girl of eighteen—and, by the time he grew up, the wild sons of the first marriage had contrived to run through the family inheritance. He was obliged to work for his living. As my grandmother had by then married Dr. Bayne Cheyne of Edinburgh, it was there that he studied for his M.D. After one or two attempts at settling down to a dull country practice, he was bitten by the prevailing unrest, and emigrated to Australia in the hope of digging up a fortune. The usual disappointments following, he turned back to medicine, prospered, and in his early forties was able to retire from practice as a fairly well-to-do man.

Of the many dim shades from the past, his is one of the dimmest. I cannot remember what he looked like, or how he spoke or moved, or, in fact, anything at all about his outward appearance. During his lifetime we children were mostly in charge of nurse or governess; and then, a young child seldom really *sees* those it lives with; they are presences rather than persons. And where some strangeness in dress, or a striking colour, stays fixed in the memory, the face of the wearer can be a blank. At least it is so in my own case. Feeling curious about my father, however, and the few old photographs of him that existed seeming to discount my mother's eulogies, on my return to Australia in 1912 I asked a very old friend, who had known both my parents in earlier days, to describe him to me. She answered pat: "The most distinguished-looking man in any room he entered." Details were not her forte, and I went away none the wiser.—For, as a young friend of my own, when pressed to admit the good looks of an uncle of hers whom *I* had greatly admired as a girl, said half-apologetically: "Well, I suppose fashions *do* change." They do, and it is not easy nowadays to see the good points of a face disfigured by side-whiskers.

I am told he was tall and slight, fair-haired and blue-eyed. He is also said to have sung well; and the remains of his flute for long knocked about the house. That he was a great reader—"*always* buying books" as my mother put it—the library he left proved; and a Bible of his which I possess points to his having been keenly interested in the Biblical criticism of his time. It is plastered in his fine handwriting with crisp comments and citations.

My mother, Mary Bailey, was born in Leicester, and on her mother's side came of farming stock. Her father was, I believe, a solicitor, who went locally by the name of "Gentleman John". I never saw any of my grandparents, but conclude he must have been a singularly ugly man. For those of his children who were said to take after him were extremely plain. Having begotten the usual enormous Victorian family he died, not much over forty, leaving my grandmother very poorly off. For a time she supported herself by running a small "dame's school"; and the majority of her eleven children became wanderers. Four made their homes in Australia, two in India, one disappeared in America and one among the Greek Isles.

At the age of fourteen my mother was packed off to join a brother in Melbourne. She travelled quite alone, in charge of the Captain, and of course under sail. Would that I had got her to describe that first voyage of hers!—she, who could hardly put foot on a sturdy steamer without feeling ill, and was capable of being as sick the day before she landed as at the start. But when young we have small interest to spare for our parents' lives before we came into them: we are much too much occupied with ourselves and our own.

However, she lived to reach the shores of Australia, and a few years later met my father and was married to him.

Being even as a child very sensitive to a person's appearance, I always felt thankful that my mother did not belong to the plain half of her family, with their immensely long upper lips and boneless, puddingy faces. She was in fact a rather striking woman. She had well-cut features, dark glossy hair, an ivory-white skin, and a pair of black eyes that I have rarely seen equalled for brilliance. And she kept her good looks to the end. I still remember how the little German doctor who attended her in her last illness, after gazing at her for some time said softly, as if to himself: "Eine *schöne* Frau!" Her nose was the feature I most envied her. It was small, straight and beautifully formed. My own, inherited from my Irish forebears, was long, thin, and drooped at the tip, and it brought me a good deal of unpleasant notice both at home and at school.

My mother had no intellectual interests, I cannot remember ever seeing her read anything but a light novel; or perhaps, in later life, when she was managing her own affairs, the mining news in the local paper. Her talents were purely practical; and there was little she could not do with her large, capable hands. As a child I have stood by and watched her whitewash the walls, or repair or upholster the furniture, or, creature of boundless energy that she was, dig a net-work of trenches to irrigate the garden. That, however, certain undeveloped faculties may have lain dormant in her seems not improbable, when I recall her love for pottering over the works of, say, an unruly sewing-machine, or a stopped clock, and her success in getting it to go again.

8

Her natural bent may have been for mechanics, a field entirely closed, of course, to women of her day. Not for nothing did she have the massive brow, peculiarly broad, peculiarly square, otherwise found only among the males of her family; and in them forming so marked a characteristic that it has come to be known among us of a younger generation as the "Bailey forehead". It missed her own daughters, but has been handed down to a still later descendant.

To these two widely differing parents I was born some fifteen years after marriage, when my father was about forty-four, my mother thirty-three. They had almost given up hope of a family, and I was passionately welcomed, for my mother adored children. Having not long returned from one of their several journeys to England, and the house my father was building for himself at Balaclava not being finished, they took a furnished house for the event. There, at 1 Blanche Terrace, East Melbourne, I was born, on January the third, eighteen hundred and seventy, amid the crashings of a terrific thunderstorm.—Until I went back in 1912 I had never had the curiosity to look up my birthplace. I then found I must frequently have passed the funny little flat-fronted house when at College.

It was a difficult birth, and both my mother and I nearly died of it, she remaining so ill that she did not see me till I was over a fortnight old. I weighed not quite three pounds, and, too small to be dressed, lay on a pillow wrapped in wadding. As she could not nurse me, I was brought up on goat's milk. And though it may be fanciful to ascribe the deleterious effect thunderstorms always have on me to the one that raged when I was born, I think I can safely put

9

my abhorrence of milk in any shape or form down to that goat. (Why it could not have been a cow I can't imagine.) In spite of these drawbacks, however, I was said to be a healthy and contented infant, who seldom cried.—In this, a complete contrast to my sister. She, though of normal size and entering the world with comparative ease, was never done wailing. Her arrival fifteen months later completed the family; there were only the two of us.

On receiving these unexpected, heaven-sent gifts, my parents seem to have fallen into a very romantic mood. To judge by the names they gave us. Though my mother had her own beautiful Mary, or the Elizabeth or Sarah or Grace of her sisters to choose from, I was beplastered with Ethel Florence, on top of the Lindesay, and my sister was in much the same boat. Ethel was bad enough, but the Florence I sheerly detested; and it has never figured but as an initial in my signature. Nor did anyone make use of the Ethel. At home I answered to Et or Ettie, at school here and there to Etta.—I have often thought, revengefully, that if on growing up we feel thus strongly, our parents ought to be made to take over the silly names inflicted upon us helpless infants.

When my sister came we were settled at "Fairfield", as my father called his house. Of this place, my home for the next three years, I have no recollection whatever. That speaks, I think, for its having been a happy and event-less time; for, as a German philosopher has said, it is the disagreeables of life that stand out in the memory. Both the disjointed impressions remaining from this early period had to do with outside happenings. The first is of lying on a floor that went revoltingly up and down, and smelt of straw. My mother, though pooh-poohing the straw, thought this must have been the floor of the brougham, where I was laid after visiting a surgeon for the removal of a small tumour over one eye. She, however, had the knack of forgetting unpleasant details. I imagine that I was probably being very, very sick. For they had no doubt given me chloroform, local anaesthetics being then unknown; and the effects of this drug on me are to this day disastrous.

I would then be about a year old. The same age throws up a vivid picture of a roomful of women, in Paisley bedgowns, weeping freely with passionate gestures. There was probably only one—an aunt who had recently lost her baby—and, knowing her afterwards as very large and fat, I conclude I must have multiplied her. Still more striking to my infant eye was the fact that the doorway leading down two steps into the next room had no door to it, was just an empty space. I do not know why this should have so impressed me. Perhaps even by then my lifelong aversion to noise had set in, and, though still without the use of my legs, I contemplated making an escape through it.

It is said that I was able to hum tunes before I could speak. And on one occasion an old clergyman in the same railway-carriage was so affected by hearing me croon *Rock of Ages* to my doll, that, to my nurse's indignation, he declared: "The little angel is not long for this world." Another hearsay incident is that on grabbing a knife from the table by its blade, and cutting my hand, I fell back in a faint in my nurse's arms. Though I was only about eighteen months old at the time, this is not incredible. For the habit

11

of momentarily losing consciousness—either from pain or extreme exhaustion—has persisted.

From the walking-stage dates the story that I once led my baby sister behind the door and savagely bit her in the arm. I can well believe it. In my little heart I must often have resented this intruder, who called for and got so much of the attention that had formerly been mine alone. However, by letting out my evil feelings I evidently got rid of them. For I cannot remember a time when I was not devoted to her; and she for her part toddled faithfully at my heels.

When I was somewhere between three and four our parents took us with them to England. The voyage on the "Red Jacket" is again a complete blank; though in its course I nearly lost my life. On deck one day with our nurse, we were caught by a huge sea breaking unexpectedly over the side. She just managed to seize the baby and hold her aloft, but I was carried away, and would undoubtedly have been swept overboard, had a sailor not made a dash for me and grabbed me by the clothes.

Oddly enough this incident left no fear of the sea behind it; I suppose I was too young to draw conclusions. On the contrary, my love for the sea and everything to do with it has amounted almost to a passion. Had I been a man I should certainly have followed it. Wherever I may be, all roads lead back to it; and I am never happier or fitter than when on it—or in it or beside it. On land a very indifferent sleeper who wakes at the least sound, put me on a ship, and the groaning of the timbers, the tossing of the waves and howling of winds seem to act as a lullaby. It goes without saying that I have never known the miseries of sea-sickness. And even as a toddler on the "Red Jacket" went about pestering for food, when merely to think of it made the stomachs of the prostrate forms around me heave anew.

From the time of our arrival in England the memories begin to grow clearer and more connected. In one house where we stayed I shared a bed with an aunt; and I well remember being wakened in the morning by her cry of: "Good gracious! The child's fallen out of bed." So it was; but I had gone on sleeping on the floor. In this same house was a lavatory—the first indoor lavatory I had seen, and vaguely considered not quite *nice*—that I was very much afraid of. For the seat went down some distance when you sat on it; and I felt it might go on sinking, and I with it, to who knew what subterranean depths. My visits to it were a nightmare, and only made possible by the tight clasp of a grown-up's hand.

From a house in Kensington I carry away my earliest picture of my father, or rather of the dressing-gown he wore—a light grey piped with red—as he sat at breakfast reading *The Times*. It was he, too, or more exactly his hands, which led us children to the Serpentine to show us our first ice. A bit was also broken off that we might feel it.—Another and more humiliating recollection is that of the donkey provided by our parents, as a treat, to take us riding on Hampstead Heath. It was behung with two deep panniers, and the idea of being packed into one of these was evidently too much for me. I stubbornly declined; and, my sister following suit, our excursion consisted of walking alongside man and donkey, safe under "Nannan's" wing.

One other memory from this time, and a truly luscious one. While staying at Clifton for the summer I was given a helping of apple and blackberry tart with "clotted" cream. The flavour of this goodly mixture I never forgot; it persisted through all the years that were to elapse till I tasted it again.

When my father and mother went abroad, we children were left in Ireland with the Henry Richardsons. He, a cousin of my father's who had married my father's sister, was Registrar of the Court of Probate in Cork. They lived outside the town, and had a large garden for us to play in. These were kindly presences, and we were very happy with them. Their chief defect in my eyes was that, being like most Irish Protestants ultra-devout, they expected us to sing hymns, accompanied by a harmonium, and listen to long prayers, while the breakfast stood cooling on the table. My aunt, too, disapproved of my mother's way of dressing our hair. Our frivolous curls were brushed straight and plastered stiffly to our heads. "Like charity-school children!" declared my emphatic mother on seeing us again.

She returned alone; for while in Italy my father had had disturbing news of his money-affairs, and at once set out for Australia by the Overland Route. It fell to my mother to see to the collecting and shipping of the numerous purchases made in England and on the Continent, and to arrange the complicated details of our homeward journey.

This time the ship chosen was the good old "Sobraon". I can see as if it were yesterday the mast that came through the middle of the dining-saloon, and the roomy cabin, fitted out and made comfortable with special sea-furniture by my mother, who of course spent most of her time in it. My sister, too, was very sea-sick, and abounded besides in infant ailments. I amused myself with my books.

For somewhere and sometime in between I had learned to read, and from now on, given a book, I needed no other company. I was well supplied with bound volumes of *Chatterbox* and *Little Folks*, and am said to have sat with my nose in them for hours on end. As I was still very small for my age, our fellow-passengers were sceptical of my ability, and would stand round while I read aloud to them to prove it.—Judging by later experiences I can imagine feeling quite sorry when the voyage of eighty odd days was over, and my father came on board at Queenscliffe, to sail with us up the Bay to Melbourne.—Compared with my mother's, his absence meant little to us as children.

I I

Our immediate destination was a furnished house in Melbourne, in a terrace adjoining the Fitzroy Gardens. This had been rented by my father before our arrival, and here we lived while our own house was building. It was a sad change from the open sea, and I have evidently preferred to forget it. All I know is that it was dark and poky. My mother detested it, and at once proclaimed it unhealthy. She was right; for while there each of us in turn, except herself, went down with a serious illness. Mine was known as rheumatic fever, but if it was, which I doubt, it had no ill after effects. I got up from it, however, very weak and thin, and had to swallow large doses of cream. Unlike the goat's milk these bred no aversion.

No doubt it also left me spoilt and querulous, and given to fits of temper. For here I remember for the first time coming into open conflict with my mother. On the subject of my clothes. In those days children's dresses were little replicas of their elders', and, as my skin was—and always has been—abnormally sensitive, I found the chafing of harsh, prickly, grown-up stuffs, round my neck or on the palms of my hands, very hard to bear. Even our white frocks were starched stiff as cardboard. But my robust mother had no understanding for such "fads", and thought me merely out to be tiresome.

One of the pleasantest recollections of these months is of a visit paid us by a nephew of my father's, Alec Richardson, and his wife, who lived in Sydney. It has nothing to do with the persons—they were just two strangers—but with the presents they brought us. These consisted of a beautiful "bride doll", decked out in satin and orange-blossoms, and a sumptuous volume of *Fairy Tales* illustrated by Gustave Doré. As the elder I had first choice, and I was sadly torn. So much so that, over it, I indulged in some double-dealing. For I adored dolls, and was by now a confirmed reader. My sister did not care for them, and couldn't read a word. Still, to say I wanted both would never do. So I worked it out like this: if you choose the doll you will as good as have the book too, for though she may *call* it hers, she'll make no use of it. This was the case; and the coveted volume, with its fascinatingly horrific pictures of inky-black forests and forlorn, moated castles, became mine in all but name.

My ruse was not seen through: for though no longer known as "Baby", a baby my sister remained, both in looks and disposition. She was a dear little chubby-faced thing, with a head of golden curls, and so shy and shrinking that she invited constant petting: the sort of child of whom

17

people were given to say: "Oh, what a darling!" and to coax her on to their knee. I was dark and spidery, not in the least shy, and found it *infra dig* to be nursed.

As we were now respectively something over four and five, my mother thought us old enough to learn "to play the piano"—an accomplishment no young ladies of our class could afford to neglect. Judging by her own distinctly wooden performance she herself had probably had difficulty with the rudiments, and so was determined to take us betimes. In the event, I think she must have felt rather like the mother-hen who unsuspectingly approaches her brood to a pond, only to find that she has hatched not chicks, but ducklings. For, leaving any question of talent aside, my sister and I seem to have come into the world with an instinctive sense for notes and tones; and on being introduced to music, in the shape of the piano, took to it just like ducks to water. We quickly learned all my mother could teach us; and soon outstripped her in the playing of her hardest pieces—Maiden's Prayers and Home Sweet Home with Variations, etc.—our little hands, even Lil's, tripping nimbly over the keys.

I say even Lil's, they were then so fat and small. Mine being a size larger were better able to tackle chords, and so came in for most of the notice. Besides, self-confident imp that I was, I had no aversion to "showing-off". Hence the laurels usually fell to me. But I have always considered my sister the more genuinely musical of us two. What barred her way, both in childhood and afterwards, was her lack of self-confidence. In our German years, when she switched over entirely to the violin, she was strongly urged by her then-time master, the leader of the Munich *Hoforchester*, to appear in public. She has told me how she used to pace the streets of Munich trying, in vain, to nerve herself to the ordeal. It was a pity; for, with her impeccable ear, her excellent memory and full rich tone, she might have made something of a name for herself.

Whether or no my father was musical I cannot say. But we were given to believe that his mother had at one time been well-known in Dublin as an amateur singer; and this my Irish relatives, whom I met on coming to England, confirmed. Though I must add that, being half Irish myself, I took their encomiums with a grain of salt. However, quite recently I came on an old letter of my father's, written to my mother before marriage, in which he speaks of my grandmother's "glorious voice", and mentions that she also played the harp, the accordion and the flageolet! So I suppose the gift came from her side of the family. Certainly not from my mother's, none of whom had a spark of music in him, and she being no different from the rest. To her, music stood for little more than a noise, at times quite an agreeable one, but still a noise; and at best a showy performance. Her ear was faulty in the extreme; and as a young child I have slunk from the room when she sang, so great was the pain (and shame) of listening to her. She had however a certain sense of rhythm. Better still she insisted, in face of our childish impatience, on regular hours of practice. And the facility thus early gained on the keyboard proved very useful.

I have dwelt on the subject because it has always intrigued me that two small girls, children of so unlikely a mother—and born into equally unlikely surroundings—

19

should have owned so many of the attributes that go to the making of a musician.

In the course of the year we moved to an outlying district of Melbourne called Hawthorn, where my father proposed to set up in practice again. What his reasons were for choosing this place I do not know: my youthful impression was that it seemed to consist chiefly of empty roads. Nor can I imagine why, considering the heavy losses he had had, he went to the expense of building. Pressed in after-years for an explanation, my mother could only say that he felt "the children *must* have a decent home to grow up in".

We young ones were well-pleased with the change. This house was as large and airy as the other was dull. For our benefit, too, the balcony had been made extra-wide, to give us an outdoor playroom. Here we kept our toys and had our games.

Two things however I found disturbing. First, the house was much too big for the furniture; or, put another way, the furniture brought with us from England was not nearly enough to fill it. And this was now all we had; for my father, it seemed, had sold off everything he possessed (except his books) before leaving Australia. As a result the rooms made a distressingly bare impression, on a child used to Victorian crowding.—The other source of discomfort was the long and acrimonious debates that went on between my father and mother. In the smaller house they had at least kept their voices down. Now they weren't so careful; and you couldn't help hearing what they said.

It was money, always money, they talked about, and on

how to economise that they differed. My mother persisted that we needed a daily governess besides our nurse. And so a young person was found: the first of several pale shades who passed without leaving a single trace either of their persons or their teachings. My father for his part continued to haunt bookshops and booksales—"pouring good money down the drain" contended my mother—and was not to be broken of the habit. To it I owe one of the few clear pictures I keep of him. I see his thin, stooped figure coming up the path, carrying a big carpet-bagful of books, which was plainly too heavy for him. Such a sight would bring me running downstairs. For there was usually something for me in the bag, some child's story suited to my age, which he had gone to the trouble of picking out for me. What they were I have forgotten, with the exception of one called *Max and Theckla*, which probably stuck because of the oddness of the names.—Long afterwards I met them again in Schiller's *Wallenstein*.

But very soon there was an end to books and nurses, the governess alone remaining. Inside twelve months I should say, reckoned by my birthdays, my father saw that his attempt at a practice in Hawthorn was a failure; and, deeply mortified—for to him failure spelt disgrace—he turned his back on Melbourne, and buried himself up-country.

In telling of what ensued from this over-hasty step, I do not propose to go back on the various factors that led to his break-down and death three years later. At the time I was only dimly aware of them; and, besides that, some of the more striking have been used as a sort of scaffolding for Richard Mahony's story. Here, I shall confine myself to the effect subsequent events had on myself, and to those impressions that left their mark on my young mind.

Our new home was in Chiltern, a tiny township to the north of Victoria. Of the place itself I remember chiefly its heat, which was something quite new to us after Melbourne's bracing seaboard. But the small red-brick one-storeyed house, into which we now packed, is still clear in every detail. I liked it because all its windows were french windows and usually stood wide open, which gave one a sense of freedom, and because it had a verandah running round three sides of it. Though our heaviest furniture had been disposed of, the rooms were uncomfortably full, and the garden was often considered too hot for us; but on the verandah we could be sure of finding shade and space.

It was here that, no new books coming in, I took to making up stories for myself. To the accompaniment of a ball bounced against a wall. For I was a very active, not to say restless child, and never sat still if I could help it. As I spoke my stories aloud, the noise I made was considerable, and I don't wonder that I was often shoo'ed off by my mother from where she was sitting.—This method of "making up" by word of mouth continued till I was sent to boarding-school at the age of twelve. Given a ball and a wall to bounce it against, I needed no other amusement. Nor did I feel the lack of companions to which our somewhat ambiguous position condemned us.

This was well; for my sister and I were at this time a very solitary pair of children. Of course having each other we were never exactly lonely; but there could be no

22

question of games that called for more than two; and we undoubtedly lost by not knowing the rough-and-tumble of group-playing. My mother however saw things differently. Hating the place and everything to do with it, she hotly declared that there wasn't a child of our own age fit for us to associate with. Now that we had come down in the world she went, I suppose, in fear of our picking up common ways of speech or losing our manners. And we did not rebel; for we had early been imbued with the notion that we were rather better than the people we lived amongst, and ourselves had taken to looking down our little noses at them.

My father we saw only at meal-times. When not out on his rounds he remained shut up in the tiny room known as "the Surgery". This was next to the front door which he himself had to answer did a patient knock, the detached kitchen standing well away from the rest of the house. He went about in a long tussore driving-coat that, however often it was ironed, always looked, said my mother, as if it had come straight from the rag bag.

Other than these, my memories of Chiltern are few and disjointed. One is a matter of conscience, and the panic it threw me into. I chanced to overhear my mother, in discussing youthful peccadilloes with an acquaintance, assert that of a certain misdeed her children had never been guilty. This was not so: all unknown to her I *had* once committed it; and the secret knowledge now weighed as heavy as Christian's pack. Not because I had failed to own up, but because I had innocently forced her, my mother, to tell a lie. Would it or would it not be counted against her on the day of judgment? The thought that it might was a terrible one; and I underwent much vicarious suffering on her account. Without however coming out into the open.

Another incident is of a droller kind. Being looked on as musical prodigies, "the doctor's little girls" were in frequent demand at church-socials and tea-meetings—the latter a sort of glorified mothers' meeting—both in the township and farther afield. We were driven to them in a dray, along with the crockery and eatables, and it was our business to help entertain the company after the spread. This meant staying up long past our normal bedtime; and on one occasion Lil was so sleepy—and so full of cake—that her rendering of "Come, birdie, come!" was punctuated by a series of loud hiccups. I can still hear the bursts of laughter that followed each hiccup, and see the crimson bewilderment on the fat little face. For she was still too much of a baby to know why she was being laughed at. From my seat at the piano I did what I could to encourage her; but before she finished the tears were running down her cheeks.—Her song was of course the hit of the evening.

Quite the most vivid and lasting impression Chiltern left on me, however, was one of colour and scent. Our governess adventured with us beyond the township, out into the bush, and there, for the first time, I saw and smelt wattles in bloom. It was an unforgettable experience. To this day, I have only to catch a whiff of mimosa in a dingy London street, and I am once more a small girl, sitting on a fallen tree under the bluest of skies, with all around me these golden, almost stupefyingly-sweet masses of blossom.

Towards the close of our stay, I worried my parents

24

by taking to walking in my sleep. Time and again they had cautiously to lead me back to bed. What provoked the outburst—whether my brain was over-excited by too much "making-up", or whether the sense of the general insecurity of things was beginning to penetrate—I cannot say. My mother did her best to shield "the chicks" from any knowledge of the facts. Let the children at least be happy, was and remained her lifelong maxim. But the walls were thin, the doors mostly ajar; and nerves frayed by heat and anxiety often escaped control.—It was a relief when my father went away. He did not come back; and we heard that we were leaving Chiltern. Again an auction was held, and strange people tramped about the house, staring rudely at the furniture; again we ate our dinner off a packing-case with a newspaper for tablecloth; and this at any rate was fun.

Our next home—my seventh—was at Queenscliffe, a little watering-place on the Bay, and we young ones hailed the change with delight. For, here, we did not just live near the sea, as in Melbourne, but right beside it. True, the house was only a weatherboard and the smallest we'd ever had; but we were now so little indoors that we hardly noticed its deficiencies. Our day was given up to bathing, or playing on the beach. Thanks to my father, who was determined that two rather pale and peaky children should reap the full benefit of sea and sea-air. As soon as we arrived he marched us off to the Baths, and handed us over to the woman in charge for our first bathe.

With this, however, her services began and ended. We needed no second invitation to dip and duck, and were soon as much in our element as a pair of water-rats. Nor have I any recollection of ever being *taught* to swim. From the moment we wakened the smell and feel of the sea haunted us; and I can still hear my father urging: "Let them go, let them go", when, towards the end of the hour's piano-practice to which my mother adhered, he saw our growing restlessness.

Set free we clutched bathing-gowns and towels, and scampered across the Bluff and down through the tea-tree scrub, to the wooden gangway that ran out to the Baths. Our parents knew we were safe in them. High palisades kept the sharks off; and there were plenty of strong swimmers to come to our aid should we get into difficulties. The water too was so warm that it didn't matter how long we stayed in. Among the habituées we were known as "the little fishes". Strangers called us "the little angels", because of the curls that floated halo-like round our heads. Also perhaps because my mother made us suits of white towelling, which stood out among the heavy, dark-blue serge costumes then the universal wear. These enclosed their owners from neck to ankle. Ours on the other hand were cut very short, leaving arms and legs free.—My pet performance was jumping from the spring-board. Climbing to one of the upper galleries and running out on the board, I would clap my hands to my sides and leap, to drop like a stone into the pool below. Then a swim back to the steps and up and off again, half a dozen times in succession.

In the afternoon we played by choice on the less frequented beach between "the Cliffe" and Point Lonsdale. And, for the first time, we found some other children to

26

associate with. One was the parson's little son, a shy, solitary lad of about twelve, who had suffered as we had from a lack of companions. He took, it would seem, a fancy to me; and was familiarly known as my little sweetheart. I had no objection to being liked, but found the sitting hand-in-hand that went with sweethearting dull work, endurable only for the sake of the presents it brought me, in the shape of rare shells and pretty bits of seaweed.

I mention this trivial incident because of its somewhat ludicrous ending. When we moved from Queenscliffe, he and I agreed to write to each other; and a number of letters passed. Then one day he put his foot in it by finding fault with the way I spelt his name. This was Stanley, and I persistently left out the e. He hoped I wouldn't mind his telling me; but it *did* look so funny. I however minded intensely. I had scrawled away warmly and self-complacently in my big untidy childish hand; and to be pulled up like this, have to hear I had been found funny, gave me a nasty jar. Angry with myself, I was still angrier with him. I didn't want a schoolmaster for a sweetheart, who treated your letters as if they were spelling-exercises; and so I never wrote to him again.——

In Queenscliffe my father once more found himself within visiting distance of the Melbourne bookshops; and though he was now a poor man the old passion proved too strong for him. I became the happy possessor, amongst other things, of fine editions of *The Pilgrim's Progress* and *Robinson Crusoe*, copiously illustrated. (He also brought back a copy of what Burton called *The Nights*. This, however, my mother was so suspicious of, even in its bowdlerized form, that she declined to give it into my hands. Instead, she read aloud to us a few carefully selected tales.) I can also recall my father setting me down to passages in Scott's novels that he thought might interest an eight-year-old. Had he lived, I should certainly have profited by his guidance. As it was, after he went, my taste ran riot: I simply read every and any book I could get. Either on the sly or openly, my mother by then having more important things to occupy her.

For, meanwhile, the shadows that overlay our home were deepening. Too frail to carry out the duties of Health Officer, with which he had hoped to supplement his scanty income, my father shrank into himself, and grew more and more peculiar. Patients began to look elsewhere for a doctor. Finally, after a severe illness, he was declared mentally unsound and removed to Melbourne. We saw him again only for a few months at the end of his life—a gentle, broken creature, who might have been a stranger.

I can't say we children grieved over his death. It came rather as a relief—the same relief, in an intensified form, that we had felt during his temporary absences. Children are notoriously cold-hearted in their determination to be happy—or at least to wall themselves up against *un*happiness—and we were no exception to the rule. Not till many years later when, with the help of old letters and diaries, I began to trace the shifting course of his life and the character behind it, for my work on Richard Mahony, did I grasp at least something of what he must have suffered, both for himself and for those dependent on him. I saw him then as a well-meaning and upright man, but so morbidly thin-skinned that he could nowhere and at no time adapt himself to his surroundings. And as such I tried to show him.

Here, however, I think it only fair to add that the person who knew me best always maintained that, in my imaginary portrait of Richard Mahony, I had drawn no other than my own.

On my father's collapse, my mother found herself virtually without means. More than one kind friend came forward with offers of a loan; but these she resolutely declined: it wasn't in her to borrow money that she saw no chance of repaying. She wanted not charity but work, and of a kind that would enable her to keep the home together. For above all she dreaded being parted from her children. She'd seen too much of that sort of thing in her own family: bereaved waifs planted out as encumbrances on unwilling relatives.

Consequently, she jumped at a suggestion that she should try to get into the Civil Service; and straightway wrote off to an old friend, then, luckily for her, Postmaster-General, to beg his aid. In reply he offered her an appointment to an up-country office; provided, that was, she could master the work in six weeks' time, when the post would be vacant. True, the salary was only eighty pounds a year, but she would live rent-free, and be able to keep her children with her. Undaunted, she, who had hitherto led the cloistered life of a Victorian lady, set about it, trudging daily to the local branch for instruction in telegraphy and account-keeping. Bravely, too, facing the loss of caste that must inevitably follow, in a community where a woman who worked for her living was considered definitely outside the pale.

Of this and other secret forebodings we children knew nothing. What bothered us were her long absences from home, where she had always been so to speak on tap. I fetched out my ball, and lost myself in story-making. Lil had no such refuge, and lived in a constant twitter of nervous anxiety. Our one mainstay having broken down, might not the other, too, fail us? Or, in her own words, when Mother went out would she ever come back? And this fear ate so deep and proved so lasting that it lay like a blight over her whole childhood. From now on she was only to feel safe and happy by mother's side.

Again an auction was held, and still more of the furniture vanished. Then came the journey up-country. This time we were bound for a township in the Western District, called Koroit. The other two travelled by train and coach. To save expense I and a seventeen-year-old cousin, who was to look after us while Mother worked herself in, went by sea, both being known as good sailors. And we needed to be; for the voyage, though only night-long, was one of the roughest, and ended with a landing by rowing-boat on the rowdy Southern Ocean.

Our new home—a gloomy little grey-stone building— shocked and dismayed us. It was all very well for Mother to say we ought to be thankful to have a roof over our heads: saying this didn't make it any nicer; and we had never yet been asked to live in a *two*-roomed house. For such it was—though, for our benefit, a couple of wooden rooms were being hastily added. The workmen were still hammering and painting at these when we arrived; the noise was deafening, the smell of paint made one feel sick. My mother was the chief sufferer; and had to set about her new and fearsome duties with a mouth and tongue black with lead-poisoning. How she contrived to keep going only she knew. But nothing would have persuaded her to report sick directly she got there. Besides, the nearest doctor lived a dozen miles away.

To me the tiny township seemed as mean and ugly as the house. It consisted of a couple of Banks, a hotel or two and a few mingy shops, built round the four corners of two cross-roads. We ourselves occupied one corner, the Post Office ranking next to the Banks in importance; for at that time the telegraph formed the chief means of communication with the outside world. There was no railway, and a Cobb's coach went through but once a day, and once in the middle of the night. Beyond the township proper lay some half-dozen widely-separated houses, church and parsonage among them. The country was flat and treeless; the soil so dark as to seem almost black.

Here, we had no garden, only a rough back-yard, containing the inevitable galvanized-iron tank and the closet. And as I couldn't find a wall fit to bounce a ball on, I was done out of my usual solace. "Making up" indoors didn't do, now that we "kept an office". It disturbed Mother, who still suffered tremors about her Morse; especially when her one helper—a youth who combined the jobs of letter-carrier and telegraph boy—was out on his rounds.—To fill the gap I took to composing "poems". These being short didn't necessitate my sitting still—could even be written standing—and nobody raised any objections to them. On the contrary. Where my story-telling brought me chiefly ridicule, the ability to rhyme love and dove and fair and hair was loudly applauded; and my productions passed from hand to hand.

Mother had an unconquerable prejudice against State Schools, and so I ran a mile every morning to the Rectory, where I shared lessons with the Parson's two children. We were taught by his wife—a tall, rather elegant lady, whom at first I held in some awe because she "painted pictures on an easel". Of what I learnt there I remember nothing—it probably *was* nothing—but the people themselves provided me with one or two unforgettable scenes.

The Parson bore a German-sounding name, and was a kindly, blond-bearded little man, in manner and appearance—as I found later on when I came to know the genus—a typical German Pastor. Being musical, he tried to improve my taste by introducing me to Mendelssohn's *Songs Without Words*, and by singing lengthy Chorals to me in his mother-tongue.—But that there was another and very different side to him I soon discovered. One day as we sat at lessons the door flung open, he strode in, and, without uttering a word, fell to mercilessly belabouring his fourteen-year-old daughter about the head and ears. The savage blows, given with the flat of his hand and in a sort of rhythm, first on one side then the other, were so loud that they could have been heard in the road. I thought he'd never stop; and sat petrified, momentarily expecting the girl to fall down in a fit. Or at least to cry or to scream with the pain. But not she: she didn't even try to dodge the blows, just sat there, with a crimson face and nipped-in lips, and let him hammer her. Till he'd had enough and marched out again, still without a word. What she was being punished for remained her secret. I could only guess she had done something to enrage her step-mother. Who was said to hate both children as much as they hated her. I walked home feeling quite weak in the legs, and far too ashamed of what I had seen to speak of it.

The boy, a tiresome monkey about my own age, was dealt with by the lady herself. She taught with a riding-whip beside her; and as often as not the lessons were punctuated by a series of short sharp cracks. If these failed she got up and went for him, with the whip. But nothing came of that either, he was so quick. Running round and round the table, dodging chairs, or jumping them, or knocking them over to hinder her, till he had her completely out of breath; and, red and perspiring, she gave up the chase.

Except for this boy and his sister, the one so cheeky, the other so buttoned-up, Lil and I were thrown on ourselves for company. The policeman who lived next door to us had a girl; but she went to the State School, and we weren't supposed to know her. We did, on the quiet, over the top of the paling fence, but she proved to be a silly thing who, though twelve years old, still went round sucking her thumb. More diverting was the view thus obtained of the "lock-up", and of the occasional drunks it housed. We were indeed hard put to it for amusement, in our miserable back-yard.

Another scrap of flotsam washed up by memory is of going to see a small dead child. She belonged to some people called O'Brien, who kept one of the hotels; and to my intense surprise lay decked out all in white, with a veil and orange-blossoms—the very image, a few sizes bigger, of my one-time beloved doll. We were told that she was now a "Bride of the Church"; but what this meant, and how at her age it was possible to be a bride, remained a mystery. I could hardly cross-question the weeping mother; and nobody at home knew any more than I did.

Another object of curiosity—this time very much alive—was the butcher's child, a teeny-weeny half-caste with a dark yellow skin and slitty, black Chinese eyes. Though only three, she was a notorious mischief and in constant hot water with the neighbours. When her father got out his whip to thrash her, she was said to take refuge in one of the carcases hanging in the shop. I longed once to catch her there; and though as a rule above running errands, I never minded "fetching the meat".

About this time I went, by special invitation, to visit a quite new baby that had arrived to a lady we knew at the Bank. "The youngest baby *you'll* ever have seen!" announced my cousin. It certainly was, being only two hours old. Its mother lay sick in bed, and I thought how nice *she* looked, with a strip of her white chest showing. But the baby! Carried in on a pillow and presented for our inspection, it seemed to me not only the newest but the ugliest thing I'd ever set eyes on. Quite bald, the colour of underdone meat, and with a face like an old, old man's, all creases and wrinkles. I regarded it with extreme distaste; and firmly shook my head when urged to touch its twitching fingers.—And there was Mother declaring enthusiastically: "Oh, what a lovely boy!" Lovely indeed! I was glad to get away from it.

But this was not the only effect of the visit. Something overheard in its course must have set me ruminating on matters till then unthought-of. For, a day or two later, I approached my cousin with the inquiry whether women could have children after their husbands died.

I can still see the look of stupefaction on her broad, mobile face.

"What on earth...Good gracious, you mustn't *ever* ask questions like that!"

"Why not?" from me, in innocent surprise.

"Why? Because you mustn't, that's all. Nice little girls *never* do!"

"But *why*?" I persisted.

"Because they don't, because it's naughty. Now let me hear no more about it!"

Even my mother, when informed, raised her eyebrows. "What next, I wonder!"

I withdrew red and discomfited, conscious that I had disgraced myself, but quite unable to understand how. My inquiry had sprung from a real desire for information—not improbably had to do with one of the stories I told myself to sleep with, at night. As things stood, all I learned was that it was advisable to keep off the subject of babies. One might look at them, however hideous they were, but to ask

36

questions about them was somehow not *nice*. So I let them alone. And in due course obtained the knowledge I sought in the usual devious ways.

On my forthright, all-knowing cousin, however, I managed to get something of my own back. She was studying for an examination, and went about the house with an open book before her, muttering to herself. Just from hearing her I picked up what she, having no verbal memory, found it so hard to master; and to annoy her would spout line after line of the poem beginning:

Of Man's first disobedience, and the fruit
Of that forbidden tree, whose mortal taste
Brought death into the world, and all our woe...

—She christened me "the talking parrot".

The mentioning of christening brings back a tragi-comedy in which my little sister was involved. It came about like this. Mother had an old friend staying with her, and in the course of conversation happened to remark that Lil had never been baptised.—Evidently, between my birth and hers, my father had determined to put his unorthodox views on rites and ceremonies into practice.—The good lady was frankly scandalised. She also alleged that, should the child die unbaptised, she might be refused burial in consecrated ground. This was something quite new to Mother—while my father lived it hadn't occurred to her to query his decisions—and the mere thought of a child of hers being thus ostracised made her bristle. The parson was drawn in; and it was decided to repair the error without delay.

The prospect of her coming ordeal threw poor Lil into a panic. In vain she was assured that all it meant was having a few drops of water sprinkled on her forehead and some prayers said over her; she couldn't be soothed and went on shaking and crying. And when the day came was marched off between her two sponsors, with eyes shrunk to mere slits and a grossly swollen face. She has since told me that what scared her was the reference to her burial. She got it into her head that being christened meant she was probably going to take ill and die. And besides this, she'd felt so horribly ashamed. That she, a great girl of eight, should have to go through what was usually only done to little babies!—At the time, I laughed with the rest; now I have more sympathy with her. While admitting that she was a particularly timid and nervy child, I think all parents would do well to pause and reflect before imposing their own odd beliefs or disbeliefs on their offspring. Young children are like sheep, happiest in the flock, and resent being made to feel different from their fellows.

One day we drove by coach to the outlying cemetery, to visit my father's grave. The sight of the mound of earth stirred no emotion in me; it didn't seem to have anything to do with him. And then, I had two private worries of my own. One was a fear that mother, who had already wiped her eyes, would demean herself by breaking down in public—the public consisting of the cemetery-man. For I was now old enough to be much concerned for her dignity. The other was the unbearable prickle and itch of crape on my skin. For the same kind friend who engineered the christening had made us children presents of ready-made frocks, liberally trimmed with this odious stuff. And on special occasions mother felt in duty bound to put us into them. I suffered torments, my very teeth were on edge from the contact, and I couldn't wait to get home and out of the dress.

This was a visit of farewell; shortly afterwards, we left Koroit. In her year there, Mother had evidently given satisfaction, and was now promoted to a larger and more important office, with a corresponding rise in salary. Contentedly this time did we children watch the packing and strapping; only too glad to turn our backs on the dismal little house and its painful memories.—Besides, the pair of us had been born and bred to the excitements of change; the desire for novelty was in our blood; and we always hopefully anticipated the best from it.

A last recollection of these days has to do with the journey to Melbourne. As before, it fell to me and my cousin to travel by sea; and on a winter's night, of howling wind and pouring rain, we were rowed out to the little ship, only to learn that the weather was too bad for her to sail. Back we had to go, to make our way as best we could from port to town and through Warrnambool's dark, unfamiliar streets; and, the house finally located, to knock up afresh the kindly old couple who had already tea'd and supped us. Though it was now past midnight and they virtually strangers—merely the friends of a friend—they received us with true Australian hospitality. Stripped us of our soaking clothes, re-clad and re-fed us, and even turned out of their own warm beds to put us into them.

I V

With the move from Koroit our migrations came to an end. The new home was to remain home for the next six years. And though eventually I had to exchange it for a Melbourne boarding-school, it was always there to come back to. In it I spent the happiest days of my childhood, free at last of unchildish anxieties; and when, of a sleepless night, my thoughts turn homewards, it is usually in these carefree, sunlit surroundings that I find myself.

Compared with Koroit, Maldon seemed and indeed was a lovely spot. For one thing trees abounded. Even the main street was lined with great gums, and almost every house had a garden, in springtime a profusion of white and coloured blossoms. Blue ranges banked the horizon, and to the rear of the little town rose its own particular hill—old, boulder-strewn Mount Tarrangower—an hour's stiff climb up a trickling gully, and a land-mark in the district for miles round.

Our own house was once more of brick, and had six rooms. It stood at a corner and looked out on broad, white roads. The garden lay to the back—and what a garden! Never had we had one like it. Here grew not only gums but shady firs, two immense arbours of yellow buddleia, so ancient that their trunks were unspannable, cactuses nearly as tall as ourselves. For flowers there were roses and the usual giant geraniums, while a cool side-garden gave us jasmine, and violets galore. But all this was nothing to the fruit. Round the back verandah hung a muscatel-vine, in season so laden with grapes that neither we nor our friends could cope with them, and they ultimately went to the pig-tub. It was the same with the nectarines, the yield, too, of a single tree. In addition, we had peaches and apricots, red and white strawberries, raspberries and white-heart cherries, walnuts and almonds. The passion-fruit we left to our elders, who ate it with port-wine and cream, and plums and gooseberries were only good enough for jam. Neither we nor, as far as I can remember, anybody else grew vegetables. These were supplied by John Chinamen, who trotted from door to door with their hanging baskets.

The fact that, physically, I turned out even as well as I did, I believe I owe to this garden. All my waking hours were now spent in the open air, and fruit took the place of meat and the detested rice-puddings. I throve as never before, and soon grew out of the jumpy, overstrung little creature I was when I went there. For the events of the past two years had been a heavy drain on the nerves of us children, unavoidably forced to live through them at close quarters. Me they had left with a nervous tic, involuntary and quite uncontrollable, that made me a constant object of ridicule, laughter being then thought the best cure for such affections. This, however, gradually yielded to a healthier mode of life; and I was spared the disgrace of appearing at school with it. Lil was not so lucky. Her haunting fear of losing Mother persisted, and blighted her whole childhood.

We both, however, benefited by the fact that at first Mother was too busy to look after us. As long as we kept to the garden, we could do as we liked. The result in my case was that I ran wild, letting out all the rowdy, tomboy leanings till then held in leash. A craze for tree-climbing was among them, and it became a favourite sport to shin up a tall fir and, screened by the branches, there sit and make rude noises at the passers-by. The swing we found awaiting us also satisfied my new bent for getting off the ground. It was slung between two telegraph-poles, and you could go higher on it than on any swing I've ever seen. I should think it was originally built for some harum-scarum boys, who hadn't even bothered to secure the seat. Nor did it now occur to anyone to do so. Standing on this loose board, I learnt to work myself up till my heels were level with my head. Mother, again happily for us, was not of the timid sort who were always expecting you to break your neck. The only time I remember her interfering was when, with the aid of a Japanese honeysuckle, I clambered up one of the verandah-posts and paraded about on the roof of the house. And that may only have been because of the unholy noise my feet made on the galvanised-iron.—Another amusement with the swing was to sit on it and twist the rope as far and as tight as it would go, then to let it fly, warding off with your feet crashes into the posts as it dizzily unspun.

42

Ground-games ranged from "house" or "shop" in the arbours, to "tig" among the trees, or "French and English" on the sprawly stretch of grass. For here at length we had children of our own age to play with; one of whom became our boon companion in mischief. Mother, too, gave up being so pernickety. My father gone, I imagine she no longer felt constrained to see that we lived up to his position. Something of this kind it must have been; she herself was by nature a good mixer.

On warm days we sat on the back verandah at a table made of an old packing-case, and played "knucklebones", then all the rage, the bones being wheedled out of the local butcher. And when it grew really hot, Lil and I would enact "a rainy day". This meant stripping, donning a few old clothes and walking about under umbrellas, each in turn soused by the garden hose. A game rendered possible because for the first time we lived in a house to which water was "laid on", in the shape of a tap in an outdoor bathroom—it, too, our first. Nor was there any fear of a water shortage. Did the reservoir fail, we had a lovely deep cool well of our own that never ran dry.

All the same this last prank might have been vetoed had it come out. But good old Susan, the servant, contented herself with private grumbles at our "mess"; and mother was seldom in the garden. In her off-time she preferred the cool of an open office window. There she sat and sewed, and sewed, for, on top of her other work, she made all our clothes. After eight, when the office shut, she was to be seen on the front verandah, studying the mining-columns of the local paper in which she now had a personal interest, or chatting to her friends. Of these she soon found plenty. The Maldon people were not in the least stand-offish; and everyone who was anybody had "called", without waiting to look her up and down.

On the whole I believe her mind was more at rest at this time than at any since her return to Australia.—Which is not to say she hadn't many a petty worry to contend with, and a great deal more to do than in Koroit. The fact that the mines on the outskirts of Maldon were still working made the new office a very busy one. Then she had now two grown men under her, and they were not so easy to get the upper hand of as a half-grown youth. The telegraph-operator behaved correctly enough: it was his uncanny ability to "take by ear" that galled her, who had still to rely entirely on the tape. But the postman—a big, burly fellow who went his rounds in a scarlet coat—thought it beneath his dignity to serve under a woman, and often let her feel it. Here, too, the lines were continually getting crossed, which brought inspectors down on her; and the intricacy of the daily and monthly "statements" she had now to render cost her many a groan.

On the credit side was to be set the knowledge that her children were their happy selves again, enjoying life as they were meant to; while she could once more have about her various treasured bits of furniture saved from the wreck, for which there had been no room at Koroit. The climate, too, was bearable: though I have mentioned heat, it bore no resemblance to that of Chiltern, Maldon lying only half so far to the north of Victoria. True, her salary amounted to a bare hundred and twenty, and it was often a tight fit to make ends meet; but she at least knew *what* she had and what she could depend on, which had not been the case when my father handled the accounts. A further satisfaction was that the transfer brought her within twenty odd miles of her favourite brother, then Manager of a Bank in Bendigo. And from time to time he would drive over with his family in a drag and four, to see her and advise her.

Maldon proved a very sociable place, there was usually something doing, and that again suited her, who in her youth had been a great lover of society. Here Lil and I had our first experience of parties—both children's and mixed, for no hard and fast line was drawn between grown-ups and the half-grown. And we not only went to them but gave them. On such occasions the office, our largest room, was cleared of its heavy furniture and there we danced, hopping round in polkas and schottisches, or standing to for quadrilles and lancers. Mother was still good for dance-music, and would tirelessly hammer away at the piano in the opposite drawing-room. She could also be trusted to provide a supper second to none.—Besides these merry evenings I can recall equally delightful affairs by day. Such as being driven by a friend's elder brother, in a packed lorry, to attend the Maldon Races. Another time the same kind young man hired one of the public coaches, and took as many children as he could cram in, for a scrumptious Christmas picnic.

Picnicking never lost its charm for us who had hitherto eaten all our meals indoors, and of a Saturday we were allowed to take our lunch out to a near-by hill or gully, where we kindled a fire, boiled a billy, and roasted potatoes in the ashes. (And no potatoes have ever equalled these in flavour.) One such excursion remained indelibly fixed in my memory—and not for a pleasant reason. What happened was this. On the ledge of a gully where we planned to lunch we found a torpid frog, and, instead of pushing or lifting it off, we built the fire round it. A sister of the young man I have mentioned was with us, and on getting home she let out what we had done. Her brother's expressions of horror, also duly passed on—he couldn't have believed little girls could be so cruel, and I, as the eldest, deserved a sound whipping—shocked and confused me. For I had not deliberately set out to be cruel, had merely wanted to see "what the frog would *do*", without stopping to think of its feelings. To hear myself slated like this made me think very hard indeed, served as a tardy awakening to the fact that I wasn't unique, and would have to bring my behaviour into line with other people's. The lesson went home; I trimmed my ways; and at least never afterwards wilfully tormented an animal.—A good deal of what passes for cruelty in children may, I think, be put down to this same unthinking curiosity. Under a certain stimulus, *how* will a creature behave? In my own case I was old enough to be stung if not to remorse at least to shame. If the child is too young for shame, the best preventive might be to give it a taste of the pain it has inflicted.

At that time we were unused to having animals about us. Mother was supposed not to care for them—though later on, in England, when a cat "sat on our hearthstone", nobody was more foolishly fond of it than she. Her early objection to them was I think mainly on our account. In our rough play we might get scratched or bitten, and rabies was then not uncommon in Australia. Nor did the present craze for house-pets exist. In all Maldon I can only definitely recall one cat and a couple of dogs. Not even the old and lonely seemed to feel the need of their company. On the other hand nearly every man had a horse; horses being indispensable in a country where distances were so great, the settlements so far apart. Our nearest railway was at Castlemaine, some twelve miles off, and if you hadn't a horse and buggy the journey took over an hour, in a lumbering, bumpy coach.——

To come back to our amusements. I sometimes think how dull life in a place like Maldon, without either radio or cinema, must sound to modern ears. Actually we did not know a dull moment. Among improvised games dressing-up and acting was first favourite—especially when Mother let us rummage through her old trunks—and a play for children we once committed to memory was thought worth a performance in a public hall. Another time we gave "Mrs Jarley's Waxworks", in aid of charity. Cards, too, were as popular with us as with our elders; and we would sit down, a dozen or so strong, to wild games of *Vingt-un* and *Speculation*, at the house of a family whose size furnished a sufficiently large table. We didn't play for money, not having any, but it was excitement enough to see your heaps of counters pile up before you. And I for one never lost my youthful zest for games of chance.

With this family we also spent many a jolly evening round the piano. Like ourselves they were naturally musical; played and sang at sight, and some of the elder ones had really fine voices. And when the vocal scores of *Pinafore* and *Patience* came out, we would take parts and sing the operas through from beginning to end.

They were the children of a man familiarly dubbed "old Tom", who was something of a character. What originally brought him to Maldon I don't know; but by the time we got there he had swallowed up a goodly number of the town's most lucrative businesses. He owned for instance the biggest hardware store, he hired out horses and traps, and was the one and only undertaker. I remember him mainly for his deafness and his profanity. So deaf was he that words had to be literally blasted into his ear, and, he replying in kind, his would-be private conversations could be heard at the other end of the street. As a driver he stood in ill-repute; none but the young and heedless cared to trust their lives to him. I was once taken out in his buggy, for a treat, to see a new machine lately introduced into one of the mines. At the pace we went my elastic lost its grip and off flew my hat. Nothing irritated old Tom more than to have to pull up in his mad career; and the swear-words heaped on me and my hat shocked and staggered me.

His wife must have been something of a beauty in her day. But when I knew her she was fat and elderly, tired out by her many children and by the scorching heat of kitchen-fires, for she was cook not only to the family but to all her husband's employees. I can still see her standing at her pastry-board, screaming orders at the servant, and apparently *always* cross. Her marked Scots speech may have had something to do with this childish impression; and no doubt long years of conversing at the pitch of her lungs with her husband had made it second nature to her to shout. Report said she came of a very good family, and that her father had been "portrait-painter to Queen Victoria". What this meant we didn't know; but we duly admired, and chuckled over, the life-size oil-painting that hung above the piano, depicting her as a child complete with pantalettes and ringlets.

Like most up-country townships Maldon contained a number of oddities, or at least people unusual enough to strike a "noticing" child. One man we long believed to be dumb, because he was never seen to exchange a word with anyone. He drove past our house in his buggy every morning and back in the evening, looking just as if he were made of wood or stone. The reason for this peculiar behaviour—whether he thought himself too good for Maldon (he certainly owned the handsomest house in the place) or whether he nourished some deep inner grudge against society in general—remained a mystery. Nor would he allow his family to mix with us. His pretty daughters lived in seclusion, and except at church were seldom to be met with.

Another interesting figure to me was the plump, sonsy woman who was our baker's "intended"—and had been for many a long day. The trouble being that she was neither single nor a widow, but a deserted wife. The couple had already waited the prescribed seven years, and were just on the point of marrying when the husband turned up again. At present they were in process of getting through the second seven, now both well on in middle age but as fond as ever. Each frequented the other's house, and she sewed and darned and cleaned for him, but no breath of scandal ever touched them—and Maldon was not a place to stand for any over-stepping of the moral law. A certain pair who lived as man and wife without troubling to divorce their former partners were avoided like lepers.—Whether our friend finally succeeded in becoming the bakeress I don't know. We left before her time was up.

Then there was the old man whose father had fought in the wars against Napoleon. He lived just across the road, and I would often run over to his little house, and there, seated on an up-turned wooden case, listen to his—or rather his father's—stories of those stirring times. When I said good-bye to him on leaving for school, he presented me with a tiny yellowed copy of a French New Testament, brought back by his father from France.—This I still have.

Tales of another country came from the person who lived next door to us and who acted as caretaker of the "Mechanics' Institute". (What or who "Mechanics" were or why they needed an "Institute" was again an enigma. Often as I was in and out of it I never met one, and table and floor, book-shelves and dried "specimens" were permanently coated with dust.) This little old woman must have been well over eighty, and was so poor and so frail that Mother took pity on her, and every Sunday sent her in "a good, hot dinner". It fell to me to deliver it; and in this way we soon became friends. She told me a lot about herself: how she had come out to the colony with her brother as a very young girl, and the straits and difficulties she had been in since his death.

But it was of London she liked best to talk, London that she still thought and spoke of as "home". Beside a tall

Grandfather's clock, with a coloured picture of Westminster on its front, I sat and drank in her descriptions of life in the great city. These were highly-coloured and extremely romantic, and, in looking back on them, I should say owed much to Dickens. At the time of course I believed every word.

Other figures flit across my mind in a more haphazard way, some remembered but for a few chance words—as in the case of the fat little doctor who went round the township trumpeting the news that his wife had just been delivered of "the finest baby in the Southern Hemisphere". Or again I recall a woman who had spent the greater part of her life so deep in the bush that she did not know what a piano was. On being introduced to one she sat over it for hours, gently touching note after note as if she couldn't believe her ears. Then there was the Bank Official who was never to be seen without gloves. He had flashing black eyes, a jet-black moustache, a darkly sallow complexion, and was said to have been born in India. In our own road lived another olive-skinned, black-haired, melancholy-looking family, who attended none of Maldon's many places of worship, and were, I presume, Jews. And so on down to the chemist's wife who clung to a mid-century costume, and walked the roads in crinoline and ringlets; and to our own burly postman who rode a monstrous erection called a "penny-farthing"—on which I was once held for a ride. Of the Chinese leper who lived and was dying alone in a hut out in the bush, I had to be content with fancy pictures.

Such were some of the odd figures who stood out for me among Maldon's two thousand inhabitants, and, it may be, helped to nourish the imagination of the future storywriter. Such, too, was Maldon, with its boulder-strewn hills, its far view of dream-blue ranges, and the flowery luxuriance of its gardens.

V

Old photographs, taken between the age of ten and twelve, show me as a thin, lanky child, adorned with long black curls. Not by my own wish, for, unlike Lil's, which curled of themselves, mine had every morning to be produced afresh. There was no getting out of it either; Mother herself "saw to" our hair. And as she was always in a hurry and had no time for "nonsense", and I detested standing still and being pulled about, my hair-dressing often ended in a scene.

I had inherited several of Mother's characteristics, and an exceptionally passionate temper was one of them. This wasn't peculiar to her, it lay in the family, and was known among them as the "Bailey temper". Not all had it; some of my relatives were gentle, peace-loving people; but, even if it skipped a generation, it was quite likely to show itself in a descendant. And though I, who inherited direct, never went so far as to dash valuable glass or china to the floor in my rage, like one young cousin, or to snatch up a knife with intent to murder, like another, there were occasions when I could comfortably have done so.

By the time I knew her, Mother had hers pretty well under control. Except where I was concerned. Or rather I was the sole person who seemed to have the power to provoke it. I never saw her really angry with anyone but me. I must have been a trying child; but the root of the trouble, both then and afterwards, lay I think in the two of us being so alike and yet so different. So bafflingly different. For the blood of another race ran in my veins; I was half Irish—perhaps even more than half as I recognised when I eventually met my father's people—and for this side of me, with its waywardness and inconsistencies, she, the sturdy Saxon, made no allowance.—On the other hand, when she tried to master me she came up against something of her own strength of will and determination. I refused to conform to her ideas of what I ought to do and to be; and the older I grew the more vigorously I fought against them. Our differences, our conflicts were endless, and went on until I left home for good. Apart, we found it easier to appreciate each other.

My unmanageability was one reason why, after two years of freedom, I was sent to boarding-school—where it was hoped I should be knocked into shape. Also, in Maldon when we first lived there, none but the State School existed.

In the interim we were taught by a neighbour's daughter who had just completed her course at a Melbourne College. She came for two or three hours a morning; and, though we didn't learn much from her, she was at least very good to look at, with her head of corn-yellow hair, veiled blue eyes, and teeth like blanched almonds.

Yet, with the knack disagreeables have of sticking, my principal memory of her is an unpleasant one. For the first time in our lives we now had "Bible lessons", that is to say, we read portions of a chapter aloud which she explained to us. These might have been both interesting and profitable. That they weren't was due to the fact that the Bible provided for her to teach from was my father's, black with his notes and critical comments. From under my lids I used to watch her as I thought gloating over these with an unholy curiosity; and I made no doubt she was privately branding him as an infidel—in those days a dread and shameful term. Why Mother, with other Bibles at her disposal, should have handed out this particular copy puzzled and angered me.— Very possibly it had the largest print, and our governess was known to be shortsighted. Equally likely that Mother, herself no Bible reader, had long ago forgotten my father's scribblings.—For all that, I never succeeded in protesting. His unconventional outlook on religion was a painful subject to me as a child, and I shrank from bringing it up even with her. Besides I should only have been told I was "imagining things as usual". So I bit back my feelings and burned in silence. From the strength of them it looks as if I were even then assuming a sort of proprietary interest in my father and his doings.

Of what I learnt in these two years a smattering of Roman history alone remained to me; all else slid by without leaving a trace. But meanwhile I was laying up a sort of knowledge for myself, in my own way. I read omnivorously, in season and out of season, and it was a familiar gibe in the family that I always had my nose in some book. And a good thing, too; for at school there was little or no time to read. Nor was I tempted to make it. A drearier collection of volumes than that composing the College Library would have been hard to find.

At home I had the run of my father's books, or of such as had survived our many moves. Among them I rooted at random, digging up many a queer specimen—to judge by the three titles that have stuck in my mind. These were *Ecce Homo*; *Where are the Dead, or Spiritualism Explained*; and *The Unity, Duality or Trinity of the Godhead?* What I made of their contents I cannot imagine. But they may at least have been useful in showing a child that not all the world thought alike.

A great find was an edition of Shakespeare. Well do I remember those two fat, weighty volumes, handsomely bound in calf, printed on the thickest and glossiest of paper, and copiously illustrated. With woodcuts, which I detested; for they would have had you believe that every character in every play was a Roman, or at least wore a Roman toga; and that didn't make sense with what you read.—*Romeo* and *Hamlet* were prime favourites; I knew whole scenes by heart; and poor Lil, who hadn't my parrot memory, was roped in to learn them, too, that we might act them together. I can still see her insecurely perched in a tree, stuttering through the lines *Thou knowest the mask of night is on my face*, while, safe on terra firma, I ranted *Lady, by yonder blessed moon I swear*, and so forth. Nor did she shine in the ghost-scene from *Hamlet*, acted by the light of a candle, with me draped in a bed-sheet muttering *I am thy father's spirit*; for of ghosts poor Lil was mortally afraid. Absurd as all this sounds in retrospect, there might have been worse ways for a child to approach Shakespeare; it at least tried to show his characters in action. The two plays I "did" at College were so cumbered with references and derivations that they stood merely for another boring lesson. Even now, the old sense of tedium makes itself felt if I turn back to them.—When I first went to school, my ability to quote Shakespeare proved a source of embarrassment to myself and of ill-will among my companions. It wasn't considered "the thing" in a younger girl. Worse still for her to air her knowledge. In time I grew wise and kept it to myself.

Three other books I remember for a different reason. These were loaned me as a special favour from the "Mechanics' Institute", and two I chose simply for their lovely titles: *Under the Greenwood Tree* and *Far from the Madding Crowd*. But Hardy's gnarled prose, together with the outlandish speech of his country-folk, defeated me. I could make nothing of either; and had to hand them back unread. It was the same with a volume of George Eliot, which, though comprehensible, I found intolerably prosy and long-winded. Perhaps not unreasonably if it was one of her later works, destined to improve the minds of the "Mechanics".

Not all my reading was on this plane. Mother's predecessor had left behind him a large number of Yellow Backs. These still lay where they had been found, on the top shelf of the outdoor bathroom; and to get at them necessitated a climb, with one foot balanced precariously on the edge of the bath. I managed it on Saturday night, which was hot-bath night, when I was allowed to take my time. A sort of Roman bath I made of it, with a plate of fruit and cake on a chair beside me, and one of these novels in my hands. Here I read *Lady Audley's Secret*, *Aurora Floyd*, and various others, including one called *The New Magdalen*, over which I had seen my elders purse their lips. Whether Mother knew what I was up to I don't know. She never came in and caught me. Only once can I remember her interfering with what I read; and then it had nothing to do with the book itself. A friend had presented her with several bound volumes of *The Family Herald*, and on these I was the first to pounce. Becoming so engrossed in the fate of some plain governess wooed by Lord Ashby de la Zouche or the like, that I persisted in going on with it while my hair was being curled. This was too much for Mother, who couldn't get me to keep my head in position. She lost her temper, took the books away and shut them up, vowing I should see them no more. But I knew where she had put them, and outwitted her by getting up before she did in the morning, and satisfying my curiosity by stealth.

One result of these sensational tales was that romance began to invade my own stories, which I was still "making-up" as hard or even harder than ever. For here I had no fewer than three solid brick walls to bounce my ball on, all well out of hearing of the office. It was however a last spurt. School broke the habit, and I did not go back to it when at home for the holidays. By then I was feeling myself too big, too grown-up, for such a childish proceeding. And so my story-making came to an end. Writing (let alone spelling) was altogether too much of a toil. Besides, it involved sitting still, when every limb craved for movement.

Of all the books found on my father's shelves one in particular had a lasting influence. This was called, if I remember aright, *A Thousand Gems of British Poetry*; and to it I owe the awakening of a love of verse, of poetry, that has never waned. Shakespeare had so far stood to me merely for action. Now, I discovered the beauty of words, the exhilaration of metre; and both proved equally heady. The old book became my inseparable companion. I raked it from end to end, I declaimed from it and sang from it; and by the time we parted, on my going to school, it was on its last legs, tattered, dog-eared, and black with finger-marks.

Throughout our childhood our religious teaching had been of the slightest. My father had contented himself with instilling the maxim "Be good, do good, and tell the truth", and with altering a couple of words in the Lord's Prayer which he feared we might misunderstand. As long as he lived, Mother made a practice of going to church and taking us with her; she looked on it as a duty she owed to his position. After his death, to the best of my recollection, she never attended a church again, being work-weary and glad of her Seventh-day's rest, and at heart one of the least religious of women. In her daily life a model for many a professing Christian, she acted solely by her own lights, and believed only in what she could see and hear for herself. As for us, she took care that we said our prayers night and morning; but that was all, it wasn't in her to lead us further; and our childish petitions were pattered off without thinking. The result of this spiritual starvation was that, when I did "get" religion, I got it fanatically, and as befitted a very impressionable age. But there was more to it than this. My new ardour coincided and became mixed up with an emotional experience, so strange and so shattering, that it compelled me to seek help and comfort from a power outside myself. For now I fell in love, desperately, hopelessly in love, with a man fifteen years my senior.

When we first lived in Maldon our Vicar was a very old man, considered by many of his congregation to be long past his duties. This feeling growing he retired soon after, and his place was taken by his son, till then curate at a fashionable church in Brighton. His father escorted him round the township, introducing him; but of the visit they paid us I remember only the two top-hats, then a droll sight up-country, that stood beside their chairs. It was not till the following Sunday that I had a real look at the newcomer—if look it could be called. Afterwards, an aunt who was staying with us let slip that he had asked who the brown-eyed little girl was, who listened so intently to his sermon.—Listened? I hadn't heard a word he said. My eyes had merely been feasting on a beauty of line and feature the like of which they had never seen—and, incidentally, were never to see in a man again. Nor can this be put down to a child's over-heated imagination. When he was studying theology in Durham, the neighbours used to gather at their windows to get a glimpse at him as he went out, strangers stand stockstill in the street to stare at him. In Brighton, rumour credited him with leaving behind a "trail of broken hearts". Yes, Jack Stretch was famed for his good looks. Small wonder that a child so susceptible to personal beauty should share the general infatuation. What *was* remarkable was its power of endurance. For this proved no short-lived fancy, of the here to-day and gone to-morrow kind. It overshadowed my whole girlhood; and I had still not succeeded in stamping it out when I left Australia, some six years afterwards.

The man and his actions I recall well enough. The face that worked all this havoc is now less easy to fix. I only know that the features were classic and exquisitely modelled, but redeemed from severity by a pair of laughing, dark-blue eyes, and a fascinatingly cleft chin. In a day of beards and moustaches, to be ascetically clean-shaven was a mark of distinction; and a tonsure-shaped thinning of the hair added a further exotic touch. He was also tall and slender. And merely to see this apparition, decked in coloured hood and bands, sweep up the aisle from vestry to lectern, set one tingling.

The service that followed had its own excitements. For, under him, we made an abrupt swing-over from Low Church to High. Now, the altar was gay with flowers and candles, we intoned instead of gabbling, learnt to bend our heads at the name of Jesus, and to do honour to Mary the Virgin. Fasts and Festivals were scrupulously observed. On Good Friday, for instance, services went on all day long, following the Stations of the Cross, he clad in his black cassock, the altar draped in purple and bare of every flower. Brought thus home to one, religion lost its paperiness and became a real, live thing; while the colours, music,

61

fragrance that embellished it were manna to my hungry senses. I threw myself into it with such abandon that, to this day, I cannot hear the well-known words, the familiar hymns, without a flicker of the old emotion.

Genuinely devout as he was in matters of faith and ritual—and his sincerity never came in question—out of church he was the least strait-laced of parsons. Gay, kindly, tolerant, and unconventional to a degree. For one thing he was seldom to be seen in correct clerical garb. In hot weather he went about in a white duck coat, on his head a shapeless straw hat, his feet thrust into a pair of old carpet slippers. But the whole family was like this. The two tall handsome sisters who kept house for him were as careless as he of appearances. They would scurry into church at the last moment, with their hair half-down or a placket-hole gaping. And their housekeeping was on the same level. The rooms were permanently untidy, the meals scrappy and irregular, all three being quite indifferent to food. And to comfort, too. The furnishing of the parsonage dated back to early days, and had never been renewed. Not having been born to luxuries, however, they didn't miss them. And as they were both devoted to their brother and gladly made do on his small stipend, a happier family it would have been hard to find.

Second only to "Jack's" ministry came his passion for horses. There was nothing he didn't know about horses and little he couldn't do with them. Himself he drove a beautiful chestnut, easily the finest horse in the place. He was inordinately proud of it, and lost no chance of putting it through its paces. I have heard him fixing the details of a trotting-match on his way down the aisle, before he had shed his vestments.

How and why a man of this type came to enter the church I only learnt later—from Grace, the younger sister, who in time became my intimate friend. He had begun, it seemed, as a student of law at Trinity, and, if report spoke true, as one of the wildest. Even then he was notorious for his feats as a driver: stories ran of his prankishly setting horse *and* buggy at wire fences and other such obstacles. But chance, or fate, led him to attend a meeting addressed by Bishop Moorhouse, who was visiting Australia; and so deeply stirred was he by what he heard that he there and then made up his mind to throw up law for the church. To see him ordained had long been his mother's wish; and she was said to have died happy because of it. All I feel qualified to say is that the law was the poorer for his loss. He was a brilliant speaker, and at the bar his eloquence would have made its mark. It was certainly wasted on a country parish.—

In Maldon he was mostly to be seen flying about in his light, two-wheeled buggy. We, Lil and I, often sat beside him. For he liked company on his drives, and was very fond of children, sometimes packing as many as four of us, counting himself, into a vehicle built for two. In this way I got to know a variety of outlying places—and some queer spots, too, including a leper's hut, at which he, the unfortunate's one white visitor, called from time to time with food and, I believe, other less mentionable comforts. It stood right out in the bush, encircled by scrub; but that didn't deter him, who could find a way and wheedle his horse through almost anything. I remember once being driven up a hill so thickly strewn with boulders that it would have been hard to pick one's steps on foot, he legerly guiding "Fireworks" with his left hand.

It was on these drives, to which I looked forward through many a dull school-term, that I fed my dream passion—for this laughing devotee, this ascetic daredevil. It had little else to feed on. Some hours of idolatry in church, certain immodest lingerings in the porch after service, in hope of a look or a word, scattered encounters in the streets of the township. The times I was actually singled out for notice by him were but three. One came from my having been left in charge of the horse for a few minutes, and Fireworks, instantly aware of the change of hand, taking it into his head to bolt, with three of us. It was the general opinion that, had I dropped the reins, we should all have been killed. For on his dash for home the creature chose the steep sides of a dam, and at one time the buggy must have hung almost perpendicular. Over this affair I was made much of; though, as a matter of fact, I had clung to the reins simply because I had nothing else to hold on to, it just hadn't occurred to me to let them go. So much for my so-called bravery.

The second incident was to me much more memorable. It occurred at one of Maldon's mixed parties, made up of both young and old. He was sitting out as usual among the elders, when somebody dared him to show that he had not forgotten how to dance. He accepted the challenge, and catching sight of me, who could be trusted not to be far away, asked if I would take him on, adding a merry "Don't laugh if I tumble down!" And so there fell to me a bliss such as not even my dreams had soared to: I danced with him, was held in his arms. On this particular evening I wore over my white frock a little scarlet embroidered Indian wrap of Mother's, in which I rather fancied myself; and on the way home, with a group of others, I deliberately fished for his notice. As a rule I was rather shy and still with him.—The next day I overheard the same indiscreet aunt repeating to Mother somebody's remark that, had I been just a little older...But I wasn't, was only fourteen, and all the wishing in the world wouldn't help.

The third memory has to do with the night before he went to Melbourne to be married. For of course he married, a woman of his own age and a stranger; and within a couple of years he was gone from Maldon for good and all.

On this night a few of his intimate friends were invited to the parsonage. After supper, some of us younger ones stretched ourselves out on the steps leading up to the verandah, he among us. He was in his duck coat, I in a white dress, and Grace, looking down on us from above, said casually: "In the moonlight Jack and E. look as if they were one." The words were like a fresh dagger-thrust at my bleeding heart. I winced, and may have made an impulsive movement to draw back; for here he took my hand and held it, and went on holding it, patting and stroking it. Why he did this only he knew. But the remembrance of it, the one ghost of a caress that ever passed between us, sustained me through many a bleak and empty month to come.

Once he had left Maldon I never saw him again. And for news of him had to depend on stray scraps of gossip picked up from others' talk. But I could not forget him, his image refused to fade; and any chance mention of his name was enough to set my heart throbbing.—Partly from a fear of what might be coming next; for such comments as I heard were seldom cheering. There were rumours of ill-health and discouragement, of a failure of energy and a lack of advancement, all sad tales to one who had known him in his prime. I shrank from verifying them.

When however the time came to leave Australia I felt that I could not go without seeing him once more. And on the Sunday before we sailed I got up very early, ostensibly for a last stroll, and trudged over to his church in outlying Fitzroy, to attend Communion. Only to find that, for this very Sunday, he had "exchanged pulpits" with a vicar in our immediate neighbourhood. It seemed as if, in everything to do with him, fate was determined to defeat me. I could have wept with rage and bitterness; and the mood in which I went up to take the sacrament may be imagined.

Now when, in after life, I looked back on this youthful infatuation, the one thing I complimented myself on was that I had had the strength to conceal my feelings. Nobody had known or even suspected what I was going through. Or so I believed for a matter of twenty years. But during the first world war Grace—by then the wife of Dr., afterwards Sir Henry Maudsley—came to stay with me in Dorset; and as we sat over the fire in the evening we revived our memories of Maldon and its many associations. Jack's name naturally came up, and a fond, sisterly sidelight was shed on the affair of his marriage and all that had resulted from it.—At present he held a Bishopric in New South Wales; and I had long ago acknowledged fate's wisdom in baulking my young desires. As the wife of a Bishop I should indeed have been a misfit.

In the course of our talk, however, Grace dropped the casual remark: "Of course it was you, E., Jack really admired." And this was more than I had bargained for. Its effect was to bring my age-old defences of time and oblivion toppling down. In a flash I was back in the old days, the old surroundings, a prey to the old misery. Again I tossed in a hot, crumpled bed, my little heart swollen with an ache that was much too big for it; again I paced round the dam, staring into its muddy yellow depths and wondering if they were deep enough to drown in; mocked at everywhere alike by the merciless southern moonlight. What wouldn't I *then* have given to know what was now so casually asserted. Even his marriage would have lost some of its sting.—Under the uprush of these supposedly extinct feelings I sat confused and silent. And when Grace went on to disconcert me still further by adding: "You cared for him, too, I think, didn't you?" all I could get out was a weak and mumbled "Yes."—I have often laughed at myself since for my inability to come into the open. After close on the third of a lifetime, and with a friend like Grace! What I ought to have said was: "*Cared?* I would have lain down for him to walk on!"

Another half-dozen years elapsed before I again had occasion to unearth this hoary episode. By then I was at work on the *Trilogy*, and living entirely in Mahony's world. But I had got to a part that stuck me: try as I would, I couldn't get it to move. I felt cross and tired and generally disgruntled. And one day I vented my irritation by flinging out: "I don't know I'm sure how I ever came to write *Maurice Guest*— a poor ignorant little colonial like me!"

My husband glanced up from his writing-table, and said in his wise, quiet way: "But emotionally very experienced."

At the moment I rather blinked the idea, being unprepared for it, then went away to my own room to think it over. And the more I thought the more I saw how true it was—though, till now, the connexion had never occurred to me. That is to say, I had written *Maurice* quite unaware of what I was drawing on. Later events had naturally had a certain share in his story. But his most flagrant emotions— his dreams, hopes and fears, his jealousy and despair, his sufferings under rejection and desertion—could all be traced back to my own unhappy experience. No wonder the book had come easy to write. I had just to magnify and re-dress the old pangs.—But the light thrown by my husband's words did not stop there. It cleared up other knots and tangles in my life, which at the time of their happening had seemed stupidly purposeless. Now I began to sense a meaning in these too, to see them as threads in a general pattern. And gradually the conviction deepened that, to a writer, experience was the only thing that really mattered. Hard and bitter as it might seem, it was to be welcomed rather than shrunk from, reckoned as a gain not a loss.—Since then, I think I may say that the natural rebel in me has been considerably less to the fore.

VI

But all this has carried me far afield. I must now go back to the child of twelve, the age at which I left home to become a pupil of the "Presbyterian Ladies' College".

Just how Mother contrived to meet the expense of my schooling I don't know, I never enquired. Nor would she have wanted me to. That was her own business. It may be that the rental drawn from the house at Hawthorn had been put by for the purpose. On the other hand, the authorities of the P.L.C. may have met her half-way. For the College, erected by those true lovers of learning, the Scotch, had been founded with a special eye to the daughters of un-moneyed Presbyterian ministers, and continued, I believe, to accept such girls at the original rates. I couldn't claim to be more than the niece of one; but his widow, my aunt, was a persuasively well-spoken woman, and I seem to have heard that she called on the Principal and laid my case before him.

Well, however I got there it made no difference, either to me or to others in the same box. We mixed with the crowd on equal terms.—And a crowd it was; for the College had long outgrown its sectarianism. Various denominations were to be found among the horde of day-scholars; and, as it had the name of being the best school of its kind in Melbourne, the boarders included the rich, the very rich, as well as the less well-to-do.

At its massive grey-stone portals I arrived accompanied by a small tin trunk, battered and disreputable from much sea-voyaging, and as ill-suited to the surroundings as its owner. For about me everything was wrong. To save Mother the cost of a new outfit—the sensible fashion of a single uniform for all had not yet come in—a would-be kind friend handed over dresses worn by her daughter at the same school, when of my age. These were as ugly in colour as old-fashioned in make, and I dreaded each fresh appearance in one. Then, my hair. The curls, thank goodness, had been judged impracticable; but instead I was cut to a short bob—at a day when every other girl sported a long pigtail. Both it and my dowdy frocks brought me a great deal of unpleasant notice.

I owed my chief humiliation, however, to my manners, which were universally disapproved of. Lacking any form of restraint, I had sallied forth from home full of pep and assurance, not to say conceit; and teachers and schoolfellows alike felt it their duty to crush me. And as, for all my pertness, I was acutely sensitive to snubs and sneers, I came in for a very bad time. Only gradually did I learn to sink myself in the mass, instead of sticking out from it; to hide my knowledge, keep my opinions to myself. Once learnt, however, the lesson proved a lasting one; and the old inno-cent self-confidence never returned. Some of my faculties may have been blunted in the process, but it was certainly to the good in the long run. For the boy or girl who goes out into the world without knowing how to conform to its rules and standards is a creature to be pitied. The inevitable trimming and shaping are best got over early.

I cannot remember ever being really happy at school. None the less I should have been sorry to miss a day of the four to five years I spent there.

The education provided was a very sound one, and in many ways ahead of its time: this I realized when I came to England and saw what was still considered good enough for the majority of English girls. Our curriculum was based on that of the "Scotch College" for boys, we learned all that our brothers did, and, like them, were prepared for matriculation and the University. Algebra and Geometry, Latin and Greek, Physics and Biology—then known as Health—none of these subjects was held to be beyond us or outside our sphere. Taken as a whole, and for its day, the training offered us was remarkably thorough and free from prejudice.

And yet how much of it was for me time wasted. Ir-replaceable time, too, for never again would the mind be so like putty for taking on impressions. I would have had entrants examined less for general knowledge than for some special bent or aptitude. With a reduction of weight on those studies for which the pupil's incapacity was obvious. My particular bogey was mathematics, a subject to which I seem to have been born deaf and blind, and quite incurable. Yet, as things stood, I had to grind at it with the rest, struggling through Algebra to surds, and mechanically re-iterating Euclid's brain-soddening propositions—only one of which, the first, I ever grasped, since even a fool could see that it made sense. All this, when a knowledge of simple arithmetic would have been enough to see me through life. Conversely, those girls who shone at maths—I remember them, in the main, as holders of state-school scholarships—brilliant as they might be in their own line, were dull and obtuse outside it. Yet we all went through the same mill.

No matter what class I was in, from lowest to highest, I sat bottom in mathematics; the butt of our merry, twinkle-eyed master. It is perhaps worth noting that my faithful companion in ignominy was the one other girl I met at school who shared my passion for books.

Unfortunately our so-called lessons in literature were most uninspiring. They consisted of a string of dates and of notes on writers' lives, which did nothing to form our taste or widen our outlook. How different were the hours spent over Latin! There, the old man who taught us was a genuine enthusiast and would intersperse the dullness of grammar with lengthy passages from Virgil, rolling the sonorous words on his tongue as if he loved every one of them, and consequently making me, at any rate, love them too. Under him, I distinguished myself.—But then, languages altogether came easy. Otherwise, History was the one subject I was any good at; and after matriculating I went on to take First-class Honours in it and English.—Though I disappointed the authorities by being placed third, when they expected me to head the list.

The principal debt I owe the College was a sound knowledge of the Bible. Originated by the clergy, it remained a very pious institution; whatever else one might scamp, there was no dodging instruction in religion. This included getting long portions of the Scriptures by heart. Every night we boarders learnt and repeated aloud a verse or verses, which at afternoon Sunday-school were put together to form a whole—a test of memory that tried some severely. It didn't bother a parrot like me; and the first prize I ever won was for Bible Lessons. In this way a treasure was laid up, the full worth of which I only realised later on. At the time it merely served to fill the blank left empty by poetry and literature. I can still remember the joy with which I fell upon the mighty lines beginning "Ho, every one that thirsteth, Come ye to the waters", and the gusto with which I mouthed them.

Over my music or rather piano-playing, on the other hand, I was made to feel very small. Banished with horror were *Carnevals de Venise* and similar extravagances; my job was now to learn my scales. I detested both them and the tart junior mistress who put me through them. After a term or two with her, however, I passed to one of the senior masters, and he proved less nipping. With him I went through the "Hallé School", and ploughed away at Bach and Beethoven, without either interest or understanding. Nothing was done to strengthen my fingers, which were of the thin, spidery type, or to improve my touch. And as among the elder girls there were several accomplished pianists, I didn't stand out. I have an idea that eventually I succeeded in winning the "Musical Scholarship"; but on this point my memory is weak and I cannot vouch for it.*

At another side of music I did better. We had a weekly lesson called "Class Singing", and here I sat immovably top. For I was the one member of it who could sing at sight or take down a simple melody by ear. Without me, too, there would and could have been no part-singing. If left to themselves the altos invariably soared aloft to join the sopranos. This class was conducted by our Musical Director, and I hadn't long been in it when he suggested my trying to compose a song for the School Concert. I gaped; not having the foggiest notion how to set about it, and knowing little of Harmony. He patted me on the shoulder, bade me learn by heart the verses he gave me, and go about repeating them to myself until I found a tune. This I did; and sure enough a tune presented itself, without any conscious effort on my part. It was approved of, and with a trifling alteration was sung at the Breaking-up Concert in a Melbourne Hall. For a first attempt I still don't think it was bad. The following year I aimed higher, with less success. My third effort was a Cantata, a setting of Tennyson's *Sea Fairies*; and all I remember about it is that it had solos and choruses, and was "instrumented" by one of the professional string-players who accompanied the performance.

The affair of the Scholarship may have grown dim, not so my doings on the tennis-court. But then, compared with music, tennis was a real, live thing to me. After an ignominious start—I had proclaimed that I could play, when all

---

* *Note:* She did win the "Senior Pianoforte Scholarship", in 1886. O.R.

74

I had done was to hit balls over a string with a rounder-bat, and some sceptical elder girls determined to put me to the test. This disgrace lived down, I set to work to master a game that offered a chance of lively exercise; with so much luck that I won in succession first the third prize, then the second, and ultimately the cup; and went out to play other schools in the College Four.—I never lost my love for tennis—the ping of a ball on a racquet still incites me—and wherever I was within reach of a court I made for it. When I came to study music in earnest, the game was frowned on as tending to stiffen the wrist. But I played all the same, on the quiet.

Here it strikes me that I have never minded enlarging on my feats at tennis. Or on the two other forms of sport that ran it close, walking and swimming. By which I mean real walking, from morning till night if need be, and keeping up with my husband whose long legs made light of distances. My facility in music on the contrary was rarely trotted out, for the reason that I took no especial pride in it. It had come unsought, and seemed as natural to me as my dullness at figures. And when, in after years, I became a maker of books, writing fell into something of the same category. Unlike swimming and tennis, which had to be perseveringly acquired, it just happened. With the result that I was more suspicious of it than proud. I certainly enjoyed the work; but there didn't seem any great merit in that. And a shadow of the old distrust has remained with me to this day. I still dislike having to talk about my books or hold post-mortems on them.

At school I was considered odd and unaccountable. Often to my own bewilderment, for I tried hard to adapt myself to my companions' way of thinking. On looking back I fancy I see one reason for this attitude. That I made good at tennis nobody took amiss. But to be able at the same time to turn out stuff like music smacked of the uncanny. I can still feel the oblique glances thrown at me as I sat, in what would have been my spare hour, over this unwanted task. They seemed to say plainer than words, we here, you there. And "there" I remained. I once, for instance, harmlessly invited a girl to write something in my album—we all possessed albums—and what I afterwards had to read was: "If ever you come down to earth again let me know, and I'll be friends with you." Oh, how that stung! For I had flattered myself I was already "friends" with this particular girl, who headed a clique I longed to join. Nor was I clear what she meant. Far from being off the earth I felt very much *on* it, thanks to pinpricks of this sort.

The Getting of Wisdom contained a very fair account of my doings at school and of those I came in contact with. It must, however, be remembered that both place and people were seen through the eyes of a very young girl and judged accordingly. This fact my early readers did not grasp; and the book was put down as offensive and derogatory. So much so that when I tried to revisit my old school I was refused admittance, and had to content myself with peering through cracks in the paling-fence.

The one episode in the story I deliberately weakened was my headstrong fancy for the girl there called "Evelyn". To have touched this in other than lightly would have been out of keeping with the tone of the book. The real thing was neither light nor amusing. It stirred me to my depths, rousing feelings I hadn't known I possessed, and leaving behind it a heartache as cruel as my first. Along with the new and bitter realisation that to live meant to change. No matter how fast one clung, how jealously one tried to stem the flow, in time all things changed and passed.

In those days school-authorities had not begun to look with jaundiced eyes on girlish intimacies. We might indulge them as we chose; and, even when it must have been clear to the blindest where I was heading, the two of us continued to share a room. Some may see in my infatuation merely an overflow of feelings that had been denied a normal outlet. But there was more in it than that. The attraction this girl had for me was so strong that few others have surpassed it. Nor did it exist on my side only. The affinity was mutual; and that is harder to understand. For she was eighteen and grown-up, and I but a skinny little half-grown.

While it lasted I was as blissfully happy as a mortal could be who lived with one eye on the clock, begrudging each day that went by, and filled with misgivings about the future. For this was Evelyn's last year at school, and her people only waited for it to end, to snatch her from me and launch her in a world where there would be no room for me.—And so it happened. Except that it wasn't she who defaulted, it was I who fell away. She went to considerable lengths to keep things going. But I felt myself an interloper in her family-circle, a sort of pariah dog among her new and stylish friends, I poor, and unsuitably dressed, and always on the watch for slights or patronage. Besides, it was small joy to me to share her. I wanted to have her to myself, by herself, and if I couldn't, then I didn't want her at all. And so we gradually drifted apart.

She stood, however, among the group that assembled on the Williamstown pier to bid us good-bye when we sailed for England. And in the cabin I found a parting gift in the shape of a princely box of *Maria Farina*, "to help you through the voyage". Its contents lasted me for years, and spun a sort of invisible thread between us; for at any time a fresh whiff of the scent was enough to bring her back, together with the gloriously happy and gloriously unhappy memories of the old days.

I never completely lost sight of her. After her marriage she eventually settled in London, and now and again we met. But an Evelyn married, and living in a whirl, bore little likeness to the girl I had loved. If I wanted to recover *her*, I had to fish out one of the old photographs and see her as I then knew her, with her laughing, provocative eyes—dark, velvety eyes under a thatch of sunlit hair—and altogether so lovely that she could pass nowhere unnoticed. I remember how, at a public prize-giving, as she went up to the platform, an old Scotchwoman in the audience was heard to murmur, almost tearfully; "Aye, but *she's* bonny!"

When we met we carefully avoided the past. Once only, I think, was it touched on, when she told me that she had chosen the woman who became her lifelong companion because of a fancied resemblance to me. And then it was I who shied off the subject. Nor do I know what she thought of the portrait I had drawn of her—or the tombstone I had erected to her memory—in *The Getting of Wisdom*. Unlike certain others whom I had pilloried, she bore me no open grudge for it. But then hers was a truly generous nature. In all the time I knew her I never heard her say an unkind word of anyone. Even when hurt, she was quick to excuse and exonerate. And as long as she lived a letter came to me every Christmas, in her unchanged, buoyant hand.

VII

On my youthful self and its antics I look back for the most part with a cool and curious eye. But with the raw slip of a girl who was thrust forth from school to find her own feet I have always had a certain amount of sympathy. Few young things can have felt so lost and bewildered as she. Her natural self-confidence crushed, not knowing what to be at, with nobody to guide her, and at constant war with her surroundings.

By then the home in Maldon was broken up: Mother had been "promoted" to a Melbourne office. This stood in a noisy business street, involved living "over the shop", and making do with a tiny, built-in backyard for a garden. It was like being in prison, and proved too much even for Mother's endurance. After a very brief trial of the place, she burned her boats and resigned from the Service.

She was emboldened to do this because at last there

seemed a chance of selling the big, unwieldy house at Hawthorn; a purchaser having presented himself who planned to utilise its size by turning it into an hotel. It was certainly only a chance, but, like the true Australian time had made of her, she took it, and was justified. The negotiations, however, conducted by a cautious uncle, threatened to be lengthy, and, since houses to be let were almost unobtainable, there was nothing for it but to buy another. This lay out at Caulfield, close to the Race Course, and was a small, cheap weatherboard, built on a strip of unmade paddock. But at least it stood in open country, which was something, after the congestion of Swan Street. Besides we didn't expect to be long in it.

For Mother had always promised that if ever she managed to get rid of the Hawthorn incubus, she would, in good Australianese, take us "home" for a trip. And she herself was as keen on the prospect as we were. Life at my restless father's side had engendered a liking for change and movement; and then it was years since she had last seen her English relatives. Privately she was also, I think, not averse to showing off her two girls—the one for her reputed cleverness, the other for her good looks.—For almost overnight the fat and sleepy Lil had blossomed out in surprising fashion. The doughy features had slimmed into a most shapely profile; the limpid blue eyes, now wide open, were beginning to prove singularly attractive. Yet again, Mother may have hoped that a year's "finishing abroad" would help to remove the disadvantage we laboured under as the daughters of an ex-postmistress. Otherwise, there seemed little chance of our getting in with the "right" people; even

81

though we bore a double-barrelled name, with a carefully preserved hyphen.

But until the sum my uncle stood out for was agreed to and the house disposed of, months dragged by. To me they seemed like years. Seldom have I been so miserable. I was still raw and bleeding from the break with Evelyn. I couldn't forget her, or forgive fate for making our worldly lots so unequal. The result was a quantity of doggerel verse— afterwards fortunately consigned to the fire—in which I railed my fill at life's injustices. And as if all this weren't enough, it was now thought only fair that, after the many sacrifices made on my behalf, I should at least earn my own pocket-money. And so, outwardly calm but stewing inwardly, I found myself installed as morning-governess in a small private school at Toorak. I loathed the job, and was of course a blank and utter failure as a teacher. But I stuck it out. And it was well I did. For though I left my pupils where I found them, I myself learned that there was *nothing* I would not rather do than impart, or try to impart knowl-edge to others. I should no doubt have been ignominiously dismissed at the end of the term, had I not been beforehand and announced that we were leaving Australia.

I drowned my sorrows in books. For the afternoons were my own, readable books, so scarce at school, to hand in plenty. On the shelves stood my father's pocket-edition of Scott, till then unread, and this I fell upon, blotting out the unlovely present in one after another of the great romances. I can see myself of a wintry evening, my feet on the fender, poring over the microscopic print by the light of a single gas-jet—for in those days we knew no better. Or at a solitary lunch, consisting, God save the mark, of strong tea and a dish of cucumber, with a vigorous love-story by Rhoda Broughton propped up against the pot. Or in bed, a flickery candle at my elbow, struggling through Tom Paine's *Rights of Man*.

For poetry I had a six-volumed edition of Tennyson, won as a dux-prize for English and History in my last year at school. There, we had learned a fair amount of Milton, Wordsworth, Gray, Cowper and so on; but Tennyson was not yet accounted a classic, and stray scraps were all I knew of him. From the complete works I had promised myself much—overmuch it seemed, when I came to read them. For except in the lyrics, parts of *Maud*, and the whole of *Ulysses*, which I take some credit for even then thinking flawless, Tennyson failed to grip me. I felt old and, in my small way, too sophisticated for his village maidens—they recalled early browsings in *The Family Herald*—and at the same time was still too young and too ignorant to see where he excelled. Indeed it was often the very smoothness and polish of this verse that told against it.

In those days Tennyson's name was usually bracketed with—and after—Longfellow's. And so I too would have ranked them. Longfellow I thought the world of, and had done ever since somebody presented me, while still at school, with a sixpenny paper-copy of *Hiawatha*. Here, the rushing metre and the music of the Indian words took my ear by storm. I remember, at a first reading, finding it so heady that I spent a coach-journey between Castlemaine and Maldon shouting out melodious bits to myself, for sheer joy in the sound. There were of course no other passengers, and the elderly driver snoozed on his box. Subsequently I managed to get hold of the short poems, and these too were greedily lapped up. I used to bombard poor Lil with them, in the hope, the vain hope, of awakening a fellow spark. For neither she nor Mother had any feeling for verse. Things one assimilates with such gusto in childhood are not easily forgotten; and many a line from this now neglected poet still runs in my head. *How beautiful is the rain! After the dust and heat.* Or *I heard the trailing garments of the Night, Sweep through her marble halls!* or *Peace! Peace! Orestes-like I breathe this prayer.* Or *Spanish sailors with bearded lips, And the beauty and mystery of the ships, And the magic of the sea.* Let alone the lovely refrain: *For a boy's will is the wind's will, and the thoughts of youth are long, long thoughts.* As for his rendering of Salis's *Silent Land,* then a particular favourite, reflecting as it did my own world-weary mood, it still seems to me a finer poem than the original.

In the room at Toorak where I gave my so-called music-lessons stood a number of books on open shelves. I couldn't keep my eyes off them, and soon spotted a volume by Long-fellow that was new to me. A request for the loan of it would have been looked on as "sauce"; so I took French leave, pocketed it by stealth, and carried it home. I had intended to keep it for a night only; but the one ran to three or four. It was called, I think, *Hyperion*, and included a translation of E. T. A. Hoffmann's *Kreisleriana*, purporting to relate the musical sufferings of a certain Kapellmeister Johannes Kreisler. Nothing like them had ever come my way, and they so intrigued me that in bed at night I surreptitiously copied

84

out chapter after chapter. The old exercise book containing them still exists; and I wonder alike at my zeal and at the ugliness of my huge, untidy hand.—Such was my earliest contact with a writer of the Romantic School.

Browning was then read only by the few: the first I heard of him was at a lecture given at the time of his death. And deeply as the speaker regretted this, he seemed to regret still more the publication of a sonnet containing the words "spitting from lips". What else he said left no impression: this was the one fact that stuck. And years after, when the opportunity came, I turned up back numbers of the *Athenæum* in search of the offending poem. By that time I was a fervid Browningite, and need hardly specify with whom my sympathies lay.

Even the most leaden-footed months, however, can be relied on to pass, and the day at length came when we stood on the deck of an outgoing steamer, waving farewell to relatives and friends. "Back in a year" was the promise and the slogan with which we parted; some of the more radical home-lovers doubting if we should hold it out abroad for even so long. As a matter of fact, save for a flying six-weeks' visit, to test my memories, I never saw Australia again.

Everything to do with this first long sea-voyage, for the one made as a small child hardly counted, remains indelibly fixed in my mind—from the moment I went below and caught a whiff of the exciting blend of bilge-water and varnish, inseparable from a ship that has lain hermetically sealed in port. And, my sense of smell being second to none, I have only to meet this particular one again to be back on the little eight-thousand-ton *Ormuz*—then by the way the newest and finest of her line—flitting gleefully from one discovery to another. The pleasure of teak to the feet; the imposing sight of a tropical thunderstorm at sea, or how the first sun-rays patched the surface with green and crimson—both effects studied by a head thrust from a porthole—and the never-staling joy of running up on deck of a morning, to find only live and dancing water around one. It is no exaggeration to say that I was in my element. Life on shipboard always has seemed to come natural to me.

I had plenty of chances, too, to prove my mettle as a sailor. For Mother, tempted by the offer of a five-berthed cabin for three, had taken one far astern. She, poor thing, suffered atrociously in consequence, and Lil also was very sick. I felt no qualms, and appropriated a bunk lying athwart the ship, so that every time she rolled it was a pitch for me—and the *Ormuz* had a name for "rolling like an old tub". I can still see the stewardess's sceptical face as she unmade the bed she had prepared. (So, in after years, must a purser have eyed a nephew of mine who, on crossing to America, asked to be transferred from amid-ships, because he wasn't "getting enough of the motion".) There I lay at ease, clambering down only to minister to one of the sufferers, and regarding without concern the dozens of cockroaches that crawled the ceiling over my head. Compared with tarantulas, scorpions and centipedes, they seemed very inoffensive insects.

Nor did the fierce tossing we came in for in the Bight, which laid out even some of the case-hardened passengers, affect me—unless by sharpening my appetite. As rough

86

weather at sea never fails to do. And there is a curious side to this. For on firm ground I am the queasiest of mortals, and must limit my diet accordingly. But set me on a moving floor and I don't know what it is to feel sick. There, too, I can eat what I will, with impunity.—And the same holds good of my sleep. On shore startled and exasperated by the least sound, once afloat I become insensitive to noise. Far from keeping me awake, the groaning of the ship's joints and the crashing of china in the pantries act as a sort of sedative.——

It has often been cast up at me that I contrived to sleep through a critical night in the North Atlantic, when it was touch and go with the smallish boat we were on. After days of buffeting by mountainous seas and a port gale, the captain finally decided to follow the example of other vessels in the vicinity and heave to. This was carried out in the small hours, and for a moment both my experienced husband and the friend who was travelling with us held their breaths, uncertain if the ship was going to right herself. Most of the passengers sat up all night, equipped in coats and hats. Why, it's hard to say; for no boats could have lived in such a sea—one indeed had already been smashed in its davits.—I knew nothing of all this till next morning. Having tied a piece of string from my wrist to the rack above, to ensure against being flung out of bed, I turned over and went to sleep. I have since often wondered what my sensations would have been, had I wakened and found the cabin under water.——

To go back to the earlier voyage. Vividly as I recall it, I shall here do no more than pick out a few of the incidents that touch me nearly. For the rest, barring my inordinate fondness for the sea and the ability to stand up to any weather, I was in no way different from other girls; and I amused myself in typical girlish fashion.

One hindrance to this had mercifully been removed. Mother, with a little money to her credit—she got, I believe, something over four thousand for the house—was able to indulge her natural generosity and fit us out in style. Better still, she let us have a say in what we wore. For once I didn't need to blush for my clothes. They were now well cut and strictly neutral in tone.

As it was the off-season the number of passengers was small, and consisted for the most part of elderly men returning from business-trips to Australia. A few older women made up the list, but Lil and I were the only young girls on board. Thus we came in for a good deal of attention, by far the larger share of which however fell to her. For the first time in my life, I found myself reduced to playing second fiddle. And, incredible as it seemed, to no other than the unassuming little sister who had for so long trotted humbly at my heels. It was a bitter pill to swallow. Not that I rated my own looks high, I had heard too much about my nose for that; but I *was* accustomed to be picked on as the more important and to receive first notice. Henceforth the reverse was the case.

Pretty I had learnt to think Lil. But I was not prepared for seeing her the centre of attraction, or for the fulsome epithets now bestowed on her. By our Irish relatives, too, when we met. With the characteristic bluntness of their race they did not scruple to pronounce: "E. is very well, but Lil is a beauty." The men who clustered round her on the ship were of the same opinion, and found themselves further ensnared by a wistful naïveté of manner that went straight to their elderly hearts. Wit and brilliance were not demanded of her: enough for them if she sat still to be looked at.

As a sister, it was difficult to see her with any but a sister's eye, and to understand the fuss made of her. I remained incredulous; and at the same time very fearful lest her young head should be turned by all this open flattery. However, except for a certain pernicketiness about her dress, which till now had not interested her, I couldn't detect any change.—In after years it was different. By then she had come to take admiration for granted, to accept it as her due; and, since it was invariably forthcoming, she developed a self-assurance, not to say complacency, that often made me wince. Looking back on her from this distance I can see that, added to all else, she must have inherited a good dose of Irish charm. Even when her prettiness faded, she had only to exchange a few casual words with a person to set them—him or her—singing her praises.

On the *Ormuz*, I was chiefly in demand at the piano. I helped to provide the music for dances, and accompanied all and any who sang. Moreover, the Captain playing the fiddle and a passenger named Finch-Hatton the 'cello, we joined forces in trios, or more correctly in a single trio. This was Braga's *Serenade*, and seems to have been the only one they knew. Anyhow, we went at it time and again, and it stood on the programme of every ship's concert. Equally limited was the repertory of another passenger, with whom each morning after breakfast I hammered out a *Duet in D.* I have forgotten who he was or what he looked like: the title of the piece alone remains.

Nor can I recall the features of the man who imagined that he would like to marry me—a well-to-do Australian this, making the trip for his health and going back by the next boat. He confided his intentions to Mother in secret, but she found them too amusing to keep to herself. I only laughed, and went on treating him as before, very badly. That is to say, I tolerated him during the voyage for his liberality with sweets, soft drinks and kickshaws from the various ports; but towards the end, when I saw the climax approaching, I made myself so disagreeable that he sheered off and withdrew, no doubt congratulating himself on his escape. Not for a moment did I think of marrying him. I, with the world before me, to turn my back on it and sail whence I had come!

Besides, at this time it wasn't in me really to care for anyone. I had left my heart behind me, and, for all the merry-making, was still subject to fits of Byronic melancholy. Especially when the moon shone, and when a silver track across the water became a bridge leading to the past. On one such night, hanging over the taffrail and feasting on sad thoughts, I must have let out some of my youthful acrimony with life to our elderly Chief Officer sitting near by. For all of a sudden he hailed a sandy-bearded little individual who was passing, and said, in a tone of fatherly impatience with my moony haverings: "Miss Richardson, allow me to present to you a perfectly happy man—one who has learnt to take life as it comes and make the best of it." I don't know which of us was more embarrassed, I or the rather sheepish Engineer thus dragged into prominence.

Our only passengers of any note were Leonora Braham, then well-known as a singer in Gilbert and Sullivan, and her husband Duncan Young, who were returning from a season at the Melbourne "Gaiety". I saw a good deal of them, for they had no nurse, and, being very fond of children, I gladly helped to look after their two-year-old daughter. Leonora, by now a trifle passée but still remarkably handsome, spent her time "resting", lying about in becoming attitudes, and taking no share in the ship's amusements. She stands out in my mind as the first woman I ever saw smoke—as smoke she did, incessantly and for all the world to see, in a day when a single cigarette was enough to brand you as "fast" and dissipated. So much so that our female passengers carefully averted their eyes in passing her. I couldn't help thinking she looked rather nice. She certainly had a lovely hand and arm.

Another memory of her is a more personal one. After listening to my rough and ready playing of a song by Schumann, she said sharply: "When you accompany a song of that class, child, don't slither over your part as if it didn't matter. The accompaniment is as important as the voice." Strange as it may seem, no one had ever pointed this out to me. I had "slithered" alike through classics and the cheapest of ballads. Swallowing the reproof I tried to amend my ways, with what success I don't know. The probability is that, thereafter, I underlined the accompaniment at the singer's expense.

Duncan Young, considerably her junior, was a good mixer and one of the most popular men on board. In the current phrase, *he* didn't "put on side". Nor was he chary with his gifts. On deck of a fine night he would sit and sing, unaccompanied, to a rapt crowd of listeners drawn from all classes. He had a sweet clear tenor, and the old Scotch ballads he chose could have asked no more telling background than moonlight and the sea. I knew them well, from a volume of my father's, but I had never heard them sung as he sang them, and for the first time their beauty and pathos struck home.

Other than his singing, good friends as we were, only a single recollection of him has survived. I was sitting one morning deep in a book that had been lent me, when up he came and, dropping into a chair next me, put his arm round my neck with the airy inquiry: "And what are *you* reading, my darling?" At the same time unceremoniously turning back to the front to see. It was a paper-back called *The Mystery of a Hansom Cab*, and the cover bore a lurid illustration. He shot up his brows, ejaculated: "You *naughty* girl!" and as airily went his way.—That was all; and I have often wondered why such a trifle should have chosen to persist, when everything else to do with him is obliterated. A possible reason may be that, at my then age, I was unused to having my reading commented on. Since the episode of *The Family Herald* no one had cared, much less questioned what I read, and whether it was Tom Paine, or *Don Juan*, or a Vizetelly translation of Zola. I may have touchily imagined myself chidden for doing something illicit, and by stealth. Now, I am inclined to think that the "naughty" I found so offensive may have referred not to my conduct, but to the book. It was highly sensational, and, had Duncan

Young been speaking to-day, he might have summed up his meaning in the one word, "tripe".

When he and his wife landed at Tilbury they were met by a party of stage friends, chiefly women, off whom I couldn't take my eyes. For I had never yet seen actresses in the flesh as it were, Leonora having been discretion itself in her get-up while on board. These ladies were out to attract notice. They wore snow-white veils, heavily embroidered with fruit and flowers, which, when flung up, disclosed faces so stiff with paint and corpse-white with powder that they might have belonged to the clowns in a circus. And this at a time when a nice woman was forbidden even to damp down the shine on her nose. Worse still Leonora, emerging from below to greet them, was dolled up in exactly the same way, and hardly recognisable. I forgot all about my promise to help Mother with the last locks and straps. Instead, I stalked the troupe down to breakfast, intent on noting what I could of their expressive speech, their flamboyant gestures. And stage-folk of the nineties certainly did go to considerable lengths to prove themselves a race apart.

Well, here we were, every one of us, at the end of our journey, and the joys of ship-life were over. To the loss of the sun we had to some extent become inured; all through the Bay the weather had been cold and wet and squally. But for the ugliness of Tilbury and the low-lying flats surrounding it, I was not prepared. I had pictured the scene very differently. So this was England; England, too, the miles on miles of dismal slums through which we travelled to our sooty terminus. My heart sank, and went on sinking; and many a time during those first weeks did I wish myself home again, back in a land which, whatever its defects, was at least bright and sunny, and *clean*. Here, even when there was no fog, it never seemed to be properly day. As for the ancient buildings, continually rained on by the smuts from thousands of chimneys, I could not see their beauty for the grime.

VIII

We were unlucky both in the time of year and the district
we stayed in. It was autumn, London's dingiest season, and
we lodged far out to the S.E., in order to be near a nominal
relative. Mother had often to hear afterwards, that, had she
only arranged to arrive in spring, and had taken us, in the
first instance, to a good central hotel, we might have been
less prejudiced. As it was, nothing pleased us, least of all
our new connexions—a middle-aged cousin of Mother's
and her husband, a retired Army Major. After our lively
ship-companions this couple seemed intolerably dull and
stodgy, and as, on their side, they thought us forward, and
much too given to airing our opinions, we did not hit it off.
Actually, I don't think Mother herself found many points
of contact, but she, at least, had "old days" to fall back
on, and these provided a topic that never ran dry. We two
had to sit and listen, stiff with boredom, to interminable

reminiscences of people and places that were mere names to us. One good thing came of it, though. When, in due course, I myself began to dwell on "the past", I could feel for and condone my own young relatives' fidgety inattention. I neither asked nor expected them to take an interest in it.

Besides being dull, Cousin Bessie was of the "managing" type, and evidently considered it her duty to improve our raw young colonial minds. This took the form of trailing us through endless museums and galleries, with whose contents our guides themselves did not seem very familiar. At least I cannot remember their pointing out a single notable painting or piece of sculpture. What does come to mind is a picture of Lil and myself lagging along in the rear, footsore and cantankerous. Mother did better, having a naïve taste for "sight-seeing". She was also possessed of a stamina that neither of us inherited.

Another source of weariness was the unconscionable time needed to get anywhere, in those days of horse-drawn traffic. Did we, for instance, go to visit an uncle living in Hampstead, the journey took over two hours by bus—with the help of a trace-horse up Haverstock Hill—and another two back. Meanwhile we sat incarcerated, staring glumly at the opposite row of passengers; for our elders jibbed at scaling the steep, outside ladder, and, according to Cousin Bessie, it was not the thing for girls to ride on top unshep-herded. We who were used to looking after ourselves laughed in private; and on one occasion, backed by our uncle, flouted the rules for the fun of driving through a real "pea-souper", with vehicles climbing the pavements and running into one another, and men rushing about with flaming torches.

Here was a relative who did not seem to think too badly of his nieces. He gave us each a golden sovereign, and twice took a box for us at the *Savoy*, where we heard *The Yeomen* and *Iolanthe*. But—for again there was a "but"— he had retired from the Indian Civil Service to London, "the only place he could breathe in", to nurse an incurable asthma; and this made him a very doubtful companion. One never knew when he was going off, and, did a bad fit seize him, felt sure that he *must* choke and die. The strain of listening to his struggles for breath was too much for me, who, since the days of Lil's fearsome bouts of croup, had nervously fled the noise of a cough. In after years I paid in full for this weakness, by myself developing innumerable throat-troubles. But then, as some one has said, the sound of one's own cough is bearable where that of others is not.

Leaving our uncle to Mother, who wasn't given to nerves, we stole out and wandered about Hampstead's rural ways. I mention this because it was here that I first came upon hedges, high hedges, bordering narrow lanes. Having grown up in a country famed for its openness, I found them stuffy and oppressive. It may also be that the sense of smoth- eration they induced was associated with an asthmatic's struggle for air. Anyhow I didn't like them, and though I have learned to admire their beauty in spring, would always rather be without them.—And this holds good not only of hedges but of anything that tends to shut me in. I want to be able to see about me, to overlook my surroundings. In the tall old London house that was my home for so many years, I lived entirely on the upper storeys, well above the tree-tops. And, tracing the feeling down to the present day,

I think it accounts, in part, for my unwillingness to quit what has proved the most bomb-ridden area in Southern England. Here I perch high aloft—"the top of the world" somebody called it—and from my study windows look across the sprawly old town of Hastings and its hillocks, over a stretch of Channel extending to Beachy Head, some eighteen miles off, and in clear weather as far inland as the slopes of the South Downs.

At the end of a month we left London for Northamptonshire, on a visit to an aunt. This was a welcome move: particularly as the English country-side lived up to my expectations. Here the air was clean and tangy, we had light morning-mists but no fog, and, best of all, long level hedgeless roads to tramp, bordered by nothing more obstructive than what we then called "paddocks". The ancient village had been laid out at a time when there was no lack of space, and my aunt's rambling old house belonged to the same period. Its various inconveniences—no gas, no bathroom, no indoor lavatory—seemed homelike to us, who had spent a good part of our lives without any of them. I even came to relish the dampish, nutty smell that clung to rooms and stairways. And for all its lack of beauty, this corner of England has never lost its early charm for me. I still go back to it gladly.

Our aunt, too, was a very different person from Cousin Bessie. Mother's youngest sister and on the right side of fifty, she was a vigorous, upstanding woman, plain of face but of an original turn of mind, and full of fun. We took to her at once; and though, on her part, she may have found us rather undisciplined, and, for young girls, too outspoken, we got on well together.—Here I may add that she was the sole member of my grandmother's huge family who did not go adventuring overseas. Except for one momentous journey to Leipzig, undertaken in fear and trembling, she was never out of England. She lived for more than seventy years in the same house, and died in it at the ripe age of ninety-five.

While there, I had a very lucky find. My aunt was not a reader; her rooms were bare of books. But, stowed away in an ancient cupboard, I came on a pile of mildewed novels by Bulwer Lytton, and to me starved of print since landing they were a real feast. Thereafter I retired every afternoon to the bedroom window-seat, and sat curled up, cold but happy. I read one volume after another, and when we set out for Germany *The Last of the Barons* travelled with me. I knew it would never be missed.

Before then, however, we made an excursion to Cambridge, to renew acquaintance with our Irish relatives, the Henry Richardsons, in whose charge we had been left as children. There were now only two of them, an aunt and a cousin. The latter, having been born at the proper time, was twenty years older than ourselves, and long since in Holy Orders. Well do I remember our meeting with a small prim parson, and our suppressed giggles at the cousinly pecks bestowed on us by an utter stranger. My aunt was a sofa-invalid, never budging from her couch, and waited on hand and foot by a devoted son. The devotion was mutual; but it didn't prevent them from indulging in wordy combats, which for tartness and bite would have been hard to beat. The first such scene I was present at shocked me deeply. But

I soon came to see that it was only the Irish way, and even to enjoy their quick-fire, snapped out through closed lips and in the most delightful of accents.

Cousin Cheyne—pronounced Chain (*how* they jeered at the Cockney maltreatment of the word!)—or, to give him his full load, Marmaduke Cheyne, for he belonged to a family that went in for odd names, such as a Henry Handel and a Duke, more than one Snow and several Effinghams.— Cousin Cheyne then, in addition to his curacy, held a post as tutor to the sons of some titled personage, a Lord or an Earl; and this position, and the standing it gave him, took first place in their minds. *And* their talk: we were never allowed to forget it. Now I had already had a taste of the English reverence for a title; and having landed from Australia a sturdy young radical, convinced that one man was as good as another, had thought it very silly and behind the times. But the prostrate attitude adopted by these two fairly sickened me: why, they couldn't even mention the name of Cheyne's employer without obsequiously dropping their voices. For Mother's sake I kept a hold on my tongue. But I had many a pitched battle with the pair in my head, when I told them what I thought of their snobbishness.—And of other things besides. Their religious narrow-mindedness for one. To them the "Church" alone was blessed: had they to allude to "the priests", their tone grew absolutely venomous. I got the impression too that, in spite of their word-friendliness, they looked down on Mother, not only because she had had to work for a living but because she didn't happen to be a Richardson. Of Lil and me, of course, they openly disapproved. We were badly brought up and in need of a firm hand.

It was difficult to believe that the same blood ran in our veins, that they were in fact our next of kin. And after this experience I sometimes wondered how my father would have come out of the comparison, had I really known him. Of the two his sister—marrying a first cousin *she* had not needed to change her name—was the least objectionable, but that may only have been because we saw less of her. It fell to Cheyne to show us round and to show off Cambridge, which he did pompously and preachily, and with due regard for our limited understandings. I was said to resemble my aunt; but privately I fancied I could trace more likeness to myself in him than in her. And it was a humbling thought.— Here let me add that at that time I had not begun to analyse my own character. Only gradually, with the passing of the years, did I come to see how Irish I myself was, and for how many idiosyncrasies the Celt in me was responsible.

While in Cambridge I ran across an old friend, the "Stanly" of childish days. He too proposed to take Orders; and it was hard to reconcile my chubby little sweetheart with this tall, lean, clerical-looking youth. However he seemed very glad to meet people from the homeland, and we welcomed him as a guide in Cheyne's stead; for he didn't talk down to us. We lunched at his College, which he taught us to call "Cat's", and attended a concert which it rather shocked us to hear referred to as a "Jesus Pop". Also, finding that like himself I was fond of books, he presented me with a pretty copy of Macaulay's *Lays*.

But my most lucid memory is of something he said— and not only because it was a queer admission to come from a budding parson. Before a tableful of people, he once

owned to a fondness for reading himself so full of horrors—
Poe, and the like—that, on shutting the book, he was afraid
to face the high dark stairs to his bedroom. Everybody
laughed, I as superciliously as the rest, for I was at a stage
when I plumed myself on my strong-mindedness. Never
having suffered from imaginary terrors I classed them as
nonsense, together with all eerie and spookish happenings. The day came, however, when I was to go through
an almost similar experience, and then, remembering him,
I thought more kindly of him. It was in a very old London
house (not my own) containing a staircase which, after
dark, nothing would induce me to go up by myself. Not
because I had supped on literary horrors, but for a much
more substantial reason. But more of this in a later chapter.

On our return to Northamptonshire, preparations
were begun for the journey to Leipzig. The old trunks and
boxes came down from the attics; and, when she wasn't
sorting and packing, Mother sat sewing at underclothing
which she fondly believed would stand up to the German
cold. We started soon after New Year, the idea being to
allow me time to settle down before entering the Conservatorium at Easter.

Winter had come in with a bang; the night before
we left, all dykes and ponds in the neighbourhood were
frozen over. And as we travelled through the fens I—in
the words of Pepys—"did first in my life see people sliding
with their skates", and, like him, found it a "very pretty
art". All wore red caps—they must have belonged to some
school—and the combined colour and movements of these
little red-topped figures, flying to and fro amid the whitey-

grey country, under the level greyness of the sky, added one more vivid picture to my list.

Other recollections are of the tiny steamer in which we crossed from Harwich—except for a fat old Dutchwoman we were the sole passengers—and of our sufferings next morning. For the Hook of Holland did not then exist, and we sat for over two hours on the exposed deck of a tender, waiting to land. It was so cold that our breath froze on our veils. Of Rotterdam, too, I recall only the cold, and the damp. The churches we peered into might have been made of ice, the pavements swam with water from the buckets of the cleanly inhabitants. We fled to a big station-restaurant, smelling of beer and thick with cigar-smoke (which we thought ourselves very bold to venture into) and there sat till our train went. After that we were locked into a carriage—no corridors in those days, the guard clambering monkey-like along the footboard had he to examine tickets—unable even to see out of the windows, for the ice that coated them.

We were thankful to reach Emmerich, and to be ushered into a room with a huge *Kachelofen*, which in no time was flaming and crackling, and thawing our numbed limbs. To undress by a fire was an unknown luxury, and, well content, we climbed into beds heaped high with strange coverings, most of which, since we didn't know how to manage them, had slid to the floor by morning. Before we were properly awake the stove was relit, and on the heels of the fire came breakfast. And what a breakfast! Even to think of it, in the war-stricken period at which I write, makes one's mouth water. Coffee such as we had never tasted, stacks of crisp brown rolls and twists, unlimited pats of creamy butter and jars of golden honey. To me it seemed a feast fit for the gods.—And always has: I still prefer a continental breakfast to any other. (Though I daresay that the rawness and humidity of the English climate is better served by a more solid meal.)

Out-of-doors we found ourselves in a white and glittering world. For it had snowed heavily during the night, then frozen, the trees drooped under frosted masses, the pavements had shrunk to narrow cuttings between walls of snow. But it was brilliantly sunny, the sky of a deep, radiant blue such as we hadn't once seen in England. The people too were friendly and informal. They smiled and nodded greetings to us in passing; each with his mite of English ready to direct us, or to assist us as we staggered and slid. We were sorry when the time came to leave this pleasant little town.

The journey to Leipzig, made mostly after dark, was long and tedious; nor did it end well. Greenhorns at continental travel, we hadn't thought of providing ourselves with food; and when we arrived, cold and famished, something after eleven, and turned into the big station-hotel, it was only to hear that the proprietor had "gone home", taking the keys of the pantry with him. Not so much as a bit of bread was forthcoming, let alone a hot drink. The porter merely shrugged his shoulders and exposed a pair of empty palms. There was nothing for it but to go hungry to bed. We couldn't help laughing, though. Imagine the owner of a London terminus hotel not only decamping before a main-line train came in, but thinking it necessary to lock up his foodstuffs! *He* wouldn't have lasted long. Thus we criticised and compared, being then unused to the Germans' queer notions of economy, and to their ultra-frugal, not to say parsimonious way of life. Coupled with which went a rooted suspicion of all inferiors. It was taken for granted that servants were every one of them thieves and liars, not to be trusted farther than you could see them. And since they were treated like the veriest slaves, underpaid, underfed, overworked, there may well have been some truth in the charge.

PART II

NEW LIFE

I

The three years spent in Leipzig were the happiest I had yet known. They also stood for a definite break with the past. From now on, instead of being merely a member of the family, I became a person in my own right. And a very different one from the aimless, ill-adjusted girl who had begun to feel herself odd-man-out, and to judge people and things from that angle. Now I too was caught up in the swirl.

We had come abroad solely for my sake, and it was imperative on me to make a success of the training. Hence my comfort and convenience were studied as never before, and I was no longer expected to take an interest in home affairs. I mapped out my time as I chose, came and went unquestioned, and had my own friends.

In the beginning I hardly stirred from the piano, gripped by a hitherto unknown passion for work, elementary though this was. For having been accepted as a pupil by Johannes Weidenbach, one of the two leading piano-teachers at the "Con.", I was put right back to the rudiments, and for months played only finger-exercises and scales. I didn't mind, but Mother deeply resented the poor figure I cut, after all the sacrifices made on my behalf. She of course couldn't appreciate the relief it was to feel one's spidery fingers gain strength, one's tone improve, one's span widen. At my initial test, on the stiffest piano I'd ever encountered, I had made no more noise than a mouse scampering over the keys. It was a day to remember when I brought off a simple sonata by Mozart to Weidenbach's satisfaction, and earned a grunt of approval for it. He didn't spoil one with praise; he was a stern and exacting master, and in general more feared than loved by his pupils. Only to a favoured few, those of outstanding talent, did he ever unbend; and then it came as a surprise to the rest of us to hear how human he *could* be.

Our Harmony master on the other hand, little Gustav Schreck—the pair might well have exchanged names—was kindly and forthcoming, and very easy to get on with. I at any rate found him so, for in his classes I was something of a star. Nobody else could answer an abrupt inquiry about the key in which a passing band was playing, or enumerate unseen the notes of a chord struck by him on the piano. My companions either made wild guesses or sat dumb. Nor did they distinguish themselves at Harmony. The one or two who mastered the rules worked the exercises out mathematically, like so many sums. Under my early teachers I hadn't done any better; for then we were made to write in separate staves, and the widely-spaced notes had refused to combine. Here, where the bass alone was set apart, I saw daylight, and for the first time fully understood what I was doing.

Before I had been many weeks under him, Herr Schreck asked if I would care to join a class for composition that he thought of starting. There could be but one answer to this; yet I hesitated, doubtful of my ability to keep up with his more learned students. And, as an example, pointed to a note just blue-pencilled in one of my chords—I had put an E natural for an F flat, or the other way round. Schreck laid a fatherly hand on my shoulder. "Child, that merely proves to me that you *hear* what you write."

Unfortunately, not enough pupils, of either sex, could be got together to form a class; and so the plan fell through. I often regretted it. For when I began to compose songs of my own, it would have been a great help to know what, outside the rules of strict counterpoint, one might or might not do.

Some ten years after, at a loose end in Munich, I utilised the time by taking a three-months' course with Ludwig Thuille, then a Professor at the Munich Academy and a composer of standing. He ran me through Harmony and Counterpoint, and commended the work I did for him. But he was very cool about the songs. One or two simple *Volkslieder* were said to be "*ganz nett*", the others he shook his head over. Not on account of technical errors, but because they were too light and frivolous for his taste. "How *can* one choose such words to set to music?" he asked of a witty, whimsical poem by C. J. Bierbaum. And a diffident suggestion that it might appeal to a similar vein in oneself was dismissed with a smile. Thus damped, I did not produce my most ambitious effort, a trio for voice, viola and violin built round a poem by Nietzsche; and so came short of criticism that would have been a gain, whatever its tone. But I am always easily discouraged.—As for Thuille, it was only after hearing some of his own neat and cautious songs, standing four-square, rhythmically impeccable, that I saw how my irregularities must have pained his ear.

I have dwelt on the episode because I still think this the line in which my talent might have been turned to some account. Though none but little Schreck ever sensed it. These early productions show a knack for getting inside the skin of a poem, and for finding a tune to fit it. As a pianist, on the contrary, several things told against me. My lack of bodily strength for one, my hands for another. Amid a crowd of students all at work on the same instrument, it was easy to pick out those blessed with the genuine piano-hand. I remember sitting by one day when Martin Krause, a noted critic of music, took up a friend's—large, plump, sinewy—and, exclaiming: "*There's* a piano-paw for you!" pointed admiringly to the well-padded fingertips. My own could boast neither the pads nor the brawn. They were lean and spindly, and deficient in staying-power—as an over-long étude in sixths or octaves soon found out. Somebody once christened them "Reinecke-fingers", and, like the old man's of that name, they were best served by Mozart and Scarlatti.

But these weaknesses didn't at once make themselves felt. In the beginning all went well. I worked hard, progressed from Czerny to Cramer, from Mozart to Hummel, and there seemed no reason to think I should not reach the top of the tree.

Leipzig was then a pleasant, old-world town, with little resemblance to the bustling, commercial city it afterwards became. Such factories as it had lay on the outskirts; one saw and heard nothing of them. Life was leisurely, and not over-policed: there was little hustling and jostling in the narrow, winding streets; nor had the great park and pretty woods yet been trimmed and regimented. This was all to the good, but had its corresponding drawbacks. For in the matter of improvements and conveniences Leipzig was equally old-world. Buses there were none; a couple of lumbering, jogging horse-trams ran round the Promenade and out to the suburbs, but you got there almost as quickly on foot. The river Pleisse, too, still flowed unroofed through the town, in summer giving off a variety of evil smells. Sanitary conditions were primitive, in some of the older houses indescribably so; bathrooms such rarities that in three years I came across but one—and it was used to store lumber in.

The inhabitants didn't miss them; for "complete immersion" was considered dangerous, a sure way of taking cold; and the same reason was advanced for their habit of going to bed in their underclothing, topped by a "night-jacket". Better-kept houses it would have been hard to find—servants were for ever scraping and polishing floors, and whacking furniture—but bodily cleanliness still stood low in the scale. How low, one had only to be in the crowded theatre on a hot night to discover. They were indeed a queer mixture, these Saxons. Ugly, stumpy,

113

clumsy, and lacking in all the graces, they were yet the most musical of people. Music seemed to run in their blood: the very servants talked it as we English talk cricket or horse-racing. And it certainly was in the air. For Leipzig possessed an opera-house then second to none, and one of the finest concert-halls in Europe.

As newcomers we lived in two successive *pensions*, which gave us a chance of studying the race at close quarters. The first was kept by a couple of elderly spinsters, markedly Slav in appearance, with heads of coarse black hair and curiously flat, pasty faces. The younger had been a pupil of Reinecke's in her day, and could still cut a dash on the piano. She could also pull strings; and thanks to her I obtained a private test with Weidenbach and so escaped the ordeal of the public examination. She coached me in German, too, and having a good ear for languages I soon picked up enough to get on with. But we didn't stay long with this pair. For they were wretched managers, continually running short of money and pestering Mother for an advance or a loan. And our meals varied with the state of their purse. At the start of the month the fare was lavish—puddings containing sixteen eggs would appear on the table—but towards the end we might be asked to dine off a herring and potato-salad.

Our fellow-sufferers were a Scotch family, father, mother, son and two daughters, with the younger of whom I made close friends. A friendship that lasted till she happened to light upon *Maurice Guest*, and there found thumb-nail sketches of some of their party. This was never forgiven me, and I saw no more of her.

Our next lodging was again with two old sisters, but of a very different type. These came from the Rhineland, and were everything the Saxons were not—well-spoken, well-mannered, and excellent housekeepers. As far as comfort went, we might have stayed out our time there. But the niece who lived with them not only taught music but was a concert-player, and bound to keep herself in practice. And the din of two grands going hard all day long, in a smallish *étage*, ultimately proved too much for Mother who, poor thing, had to share a sitting-room with me and mine.—And so, renting a few bits of furniture, we set up in a flat of our own, where a door could be shut on me and my noise.

But this niece, Elizabeth Morsbach, deserves more than a passing mention; if only because she was so conspicuously unlike the general run of German women. Tall and slim where they were fat and undersized, her dark curly hair cut short above a brow broad as a man's, eyes sparkling with life and intelligence. And with manners as charming as her looks. But it was her braininess that impressed me, her learning I envied her. She spoke excellent English, and was well-read in three languages besides her own. It made her a very entertaining companion, for she didn't in the least mind sharing her knowledge. I can remember her, for instance, describing *Ghosts* and *The Wild Duck* to us as she read them—at a time when Ibsen's name was little known outside Norway.

And, to conclude, she was a rarely gifted pianist.

Having trained with Liszt in Weimar, she naturally played any number of his compositions, and in masterly fashion. But my own early hacking at the *Rhapsodies*,

115

which I'd hated, had biased me; and even under her hands Liszt's paraphrases and transcriptions left me cold. I was a rapt listener, though, when she talked of the man himself. For her woman's eye had seized and held just those intimate personal details that the male eye is apt to miss, or to think of no account. My memory stored them up, and they were there to draw on when I came to write a book in which Liszt figured.*

It was to Elizabeth he said, on her offering him a bunch of roses, that the face above them was fairer than *any* flower—a speech, together with the kiss that followed, reported by one of the aunts, not by herself. Liszt named her "*Der kleine Bülow*" because, like Hans von Bülow, she had a prodigious memory, and played everything by heart. She also possessed Bülow's trick of memorising a piece of music from the printed page alone, without the aid of the piano. This was where the massive brow came in. And, did she turn to the classics, you could almost watch her brain at work. Her very fingers seemed to be thinking.

As a good Lisztian and a free-lance teacher, she probably had her own ideas about the rigidly conservative methods in force at the Conservatorium. But she was too tactful ever to cast a doubt on them in my hearing, or in any way to disturb my self-content. Except for the "Reinecke fingers", which originated with her, I can recall but one comment of hers on what or how I played. It had to do with my old knack of sight-reading. She'd lent me a volume of Schubert's piano-sonatas that were new to me. These I

---

* *Note:* This was *The Young Cosima*, published in 1939. O.R.

romped through without much difficulty, and it was hard to convince her that I had never seen them before.——

She and her aunts were the only people I made an attempt to trace, on going back to Leipzig some years after. But inquire as I would, I could find nobody who remembered them, even by name. At last I dug up an old woman who had once charred in the same building, and from her learned that Elizabeth had married and died in childbed within the year, quickly followed by the two old aunts. *Their* deaths were natural: left by themselves they would have nothing to live for. But hers—what a waste! When there were so many other women in the world to do the child-bearing.

The flat we moved to on parting from them was in one of the new streets that had sprung up round Conservatorium and Gewandhaus. Here we stayed put for the rest of our time; and with *Mozartstrasse, dreizehn, drei*, are linked both my happiest and unhappiest memories of Leipzig.

Being so convenient for the Con., houses in this neighbourhood were packed with music-students, and rife with sounds of their trade. Our own small flat was no exception. For we were now four, having been joined by a Scotch friend whose instrument was the 'cello. I, the chief noise-maker, occupied the little *Salon*, where I belaboured the piano for four or five hours daily; Lil, then at the squeakiest stage of the violin, was ensconced in the back bedroom, while Mat boomed deep-toned, hesitating scales in the one to the front.

One would have expected Mother to be driven crazy by the ensuing hubbub. As a matter of fact I don't remember ever hearing her complain. The reason was I think that she was once more her own housekeeper, and had that "something to do" that *pension*-life had denied her. Another gain to a person of her sociable nature was that we were at last free to entertain friends. By now we had collected a goodish number; and on a Sunday afternoon, when it was the rule for pianos to close down, instruments to remain in their cases, the little *Salon* was sometimes as full as it would hold.

Of English and Americans. Foreigners were not encouraged, for we'd found them bad mixers. Nor did we fraternise to any extent with our fellow-pupils, of whom the same could be said. Our circle consisted mainly of men working for their degrees at the university. And if it had come to a choice between the two favoured races, we should all I think have plumped for the Americans. They seemed more like ourselves, were frank and informal, and considerably easier to get on with than the staider English. Besides they had any amount of 'go.' It was the "American Club" that ran the dances, and got up the delightful river-picnics and skating-parties that kept us from growing sodden with work.

The Germans thought us very frivolous. But we didn't let that trouble us. And, anyhow, their idea of enjoyment wasn't ours. When living with the Morsbachs Lil and I had once been invited to a German ball. We accepted gladly enough, but came home vowing never to go to another. To begin with, they couldn't dance, or what we understood by dancing. They hopped like pogos, and expected us to hop too—at a time when the waltz had sobered down to a leisurely stroll. Then, the men didn't wear gloves, and their hands left unsightly marks on the back of one's frock. Worse still, in the middle of the evening a heavy meal was served, with thick soups, hot meat, vegetables and so on, which disabled one for further violent exercise.

For me it was indeed a full life. For over and above all else, I was then an indefatigable concert-goer. With the faithful Mat for companion I ran from one performance to another, intent on missing nothing that might be of help to me. Conscientiously I sat through the bi-weekly *Abende* at the Con., where on-coming pupils showed their paces, as well as concerts by the entirely unknown, for which free tickets could be had for the asking. The Wednesday rehearsals at the Gewandhaus were of course the peak. There we saw and heard those whose fame was solidly established. Lion-headed Joachim, by now, sadly enough, always a shade off his note; Clara Schumann, an old woman in bonnet and mantle, led deferentially to the piano by Reinecke himself, now reduced to having her music set before her; the lank-haired Belgian violinist Ysaye, and our own superb leader, Petri, are among those that stand out in my memory. Together with a fiery-headed youth named Busoni, who had somehow contrived to worm his way into the sacred precincts. For as a rule the "moderns" were rigorously excluded. If you wanted to hear, say, Eugen d'Albert or Sophie Menter in their master's Concertos, or to get some idea of Berlioz, you repaired to the draughty *Albert-halle*, where the *Liszt-Verein* housed.

The Germans believed in providing music with its appropriate atmosphere. The Bach Motets were performed in Bach's own *Thomaskirche*; and, after that, any other

119

background seemed incongruous. Nor have the *Passions* and great Oratorios ever made the impression they did in some dim old Leipzig church. The Gewandhaus had its own special little hall for chamber-music, with acoustics so perfect that not the lightest tone was lost. Here, every Saturday evening our leading instrumentalists combined in Haydn, Mozart, Beethoven. These were the only concerts I wilfully shirked, not being then grown to chamber-music. And it was perhaps just as well; for I came to it fresh and unsurfeited later in life, when I was much better able to judge of it.—To-day I prefer it to any other.

Somewhere about this time Mother went to England on business, taking the inseparable Lil with her, and also Mat, who was bound for Scotland. I stayed behind in charge of a friend, and to her flat I and my piano were transferred.

Mrs F., as I will call her, was a person whose case roused a great deal of sympathy. For her husband, after dragging her to Leipzig in order that *he* might study music, had run off with another woman—actually the girl who was their servant—leaving his wife to support herself and three young children. This she did by teaching English and letting a couple of her rooms. One stood empty at the moment, and according to kind-hearted Mother was just the place for me. It wouldn't have been my choice, for I found Mrs F. distinctly formidable. From her style of dress on. Very tall and commanding, she made herself more so by going about garbed in a loose white hanging robe, held together by a cord at the waist. In addition she had a pair of the coldest, most disconcerting eyes I'd ever had to face: they seemed to bore right through you. Still worse, she was one of those people who pride themselves on their plain-spokenness, on saying exactly what they think, regardless of their hearers' tender spots. And her tongue bit like a lash. Before I had been long there I began to feel a sneaking pity for the errant husband.

The morning after my arrival I had a specimen of her tactlessness. She came sailing into the room where I and the other boarder sat at breakfast, and, without as much as a good-morning, and before me a total stranger, marched up to my companion, thrust her hand down his neck, pulled out his collar and rudely examined the inside of it. Slapping it back with a: "Herr Z., you've actually put that *same* one on again! Didn't I tell you yesterday it wasn't fit to wear?" The meek and shabby little Norwegian Professor, who looked as if he mightn't own all too many collars, went very red, but made no reply. I felt myself blushing with and for him.

A day or two later I was the victim. The door of the room where I practised was thrown open, and sticking her head in Mrs F. announced: "You know you're *much* too good for that sort of thing!"

Like the Professor I couldn't find anything to say, hotly as I resented both her interference and her tone. *That* sort of thing, indeed! For I had just finished a particularly good morning's work on Schumann's *Waldscenen*, which I flattered myself I'd at last got perfect in every detail. If this was typical of her attitude to music, no wonder the husband had fled. One could even understand his turning to a simple servant girl.—As for presuming to judge what or what not *I* might be good for, how could she, when she hardly knew me?

Yet another of her pronouncements has stuck in my memory, though for a different reason.

Like us she was at home to friends on Sunday, and I found several of our own there. But her circle was wider than ours, for, having studied at Cambridge, she was better able to talk shop. After her visitors had gone, however, she would amuse herself by pulling them to pieces. And on one such afternoon she wound up by declaring: "Take my word for it, there's more in that quiet young fellow who sat in the corner behind the piano than in all the rest of them rolled together."

My eyes too had occasionally wandered to the person in question. I had noticed his silence, broken only if he was directly addressed, referred to, for the most part, to settle some point of which the others were unsure. Beyond that, all I recalled was a pair of pleasant blue eyes behind spectacles, and legs so long that they were awkward to dispose of.—His name it seemed was Robertson, and he came from Glasgow.

I met him again on the Tennis Courts, more rarely at a dance. But he was too shortsighted to be a good player, and I was out for a hard game. Nor did he dance well.

Our acquaintance flagged until he heard that Mat and I were planning to go to Norway for the summer vacation. Then he came out of his shell to ask a favour. Would I, if in Christiania, inquire whether such a thing as a copy

123

of Ibsen's first play, *Catilina*, was still to be had there. He possessed all the other plays, and was most anxious to complete the set. Flattered at being entrusted with the commission, I swallowed my doubts and promised to see what I could do.

Difficulties with the language I didn't need to fear, having discovered on a previous visit with the family that virtually nine out of every ten Norwegians spoke English. I ought however to have added the proviso: if we ever got there. For it would be my first experience of travelling on the continent without Mother, and I wasn't at all sure of myself as a guide. Neither were we flush of money. Our respective parents, who disapproved, had each forked out ten pounds, announcing that if we couldn't make do on it we must come back home. And Mat was even weaker than I at arithmetic. I can still see the pair of us sitting in a railway-carriage, doling out marks and pfennigs to each other in kind, equally incapable of squaring accounts on paper.

None the less we managed somehow, and, incredible as it may now sound, went and came for this meagre sum, which had to cover our fares, a night each way in Berlin, and between two and three weeks on the lovely wooded hills above the Christiania Fjord.

Being young and strong, we made light of discomforts—even Mat, who was a poor traveller and suffered both from train and sea-sickness. Many a time did we afterwards laugh over the good money wasted in Copenhagen. There, feeling rather gay at having got so far without mishap, we did the grand, and regaled ourselves in one of the town's finest restaurants. With disastrous consequences for her.

We had a very rough crossing to Christiania, and the little boat pitched and wallowed. Mat of course vanished straightway into the depths, and I saw no more of her till we landed next morning. Nor did the other passengers fare much better. One by one they slunk below till nobody but myself remained on deck. I was wandering disconsolately about, in search of a dry place, when the Captain spotted me from the bridge and sent a sailor down with a voluminous oilskin. He also recommended me to avoid the Ladies' Cabin and to content myself with a settee in the Dining Saloon. This I did, the only female among thirty or forty men, stretched out round the sofas heel to head and head to heel.

As the spice of life has been said to consist of its details, here is yet another to do with this occasion. While a handful of passengers were still on their feet, one of them, an inquisitive old German, came up to me and asked, with truly German condescension: "And what are *you* reading, mein Fräulein?" I held the book out for him to see—it was a little volume of *Reclam*, entitled *Faust*. He took one look at it, ejaculated: "*Ach, du mein Gott!*" and lurched tipsily away. Roughly and rudely rendered, his words did duty for "*My Gawd!*"—and, nowadays, I should be of the same opinion.

To go back to *Catilina*. At the *pension* where we stayed I was fortunate enough to run across one of Christiania's leading booksellers. This person no sooner heard of my quest than, with true Norwegian kindliness, he made it his own. And though he shook his head, thinking it extremely improbable that the missing volume would come to light, he went to the trouble of telephoning any and every bookshop where a stray copy might perhaps still lurk. But without success: *Catilina* had evidently shared the lot of most first books and ended as pulp. This I duly wrote to Mr Robertson, regretting my failure. In reply came a very friendly note, thanking me for the trouble that hadn't been mine, and asking if, as a small return, I would accept a ticket for the Cycle of Wagner's works, announced by the theatre for the autumn.

Would I not indeed, I jumped at the offer. For it meant not only hearing *all* the operas, and in the order in which they were written, but from a comfortable, reserved seat on the ground-floor. Myself I couldn't have afforded to go to more than one or two of them, after a fight for a place in the top gallery. The fact being that the Conservatorium did not consider opera essential to our training, and so we enjoyed no privileges. Whereas university students were able to book seats in the *Parterre*, for the modest sum of one and six.

Here then, throughout the autumn, I sat twice weekly at my new friend's side, drinking in one after another of the great works, from *Die Feen* on. With the exception of *Parsifal*, which Frau Cosima still jealously guarded as Bayreuth's sole property.

Here, too, it can be said that my musical education really began. For the first time I was in touch with someone who didn't divide music up into categories—like the Con., like everyone else I'd known—but regarded it from a much wider standpoint, and as a whole. The generosity, too, with which he shared his knowledge was something to be remembered. Nor did he ever talk down to one. Quick to respond where I didn't scent patronage, I made the most of my opportunity, and, as we walked the *foyer* between the acts, plied him with questions.

Of opera he had made a special study; even as a lad spending his pocket-money on Boosey's cheap piano-scores, to get some light on its development. These he managed to struggle through, though nothing of a pianist, but Wagner was beyond him, dearly as he would have liked to know more of the works before hearing them. At this I ventured to suggest that I might be of use to him. He hailed the proposal, I lugged the weighty volumes from Klemm's Lending Library, and, on those evenings when we weren't at the theatre, we sat together at my piano, poring over *Tristan* or the *Ring*, tracking down "motives" and digging out connexions.

Nor did our comradeship end with the Wagner Cycle. For by that time winter had set in, with its usual severity, and all the ponds in the neighbourhood were bearing. At last even the Pleisse was pronounced safe, and it then turned out that, though he couldn't compete with the Canadians in fancy-steps, he was a capital long-distance skater, having served his apprenticeship on the vast Scotch lochs. Rough ice held no traps for him—or for the beginner he supported.

A further bond between us was the discovery that I too loved books. And, since coming to Leipzig, had had as good as none; my only source being a wretched English Library, consisting of obsolete novels. To this state of things he soon put an end. For behind him he had the immense University Library, from which he could borrow at will. Henceforth I had only to mention a book, or express an interest in one he told me of, and it was mine. The old passion re-asserted itself, every chink of my spare time went in reading; and, thanks to him and his suggestions, my range widened, my judgment improved.—I can still see myself with a volume of, say, Renan or Tolstoi propped open on the music-stand, while I ploughed through the needful but soul-deadening scales and exercises.

And so things went on, happily and thoughtlessly, till we were pulled up with a jerk. Some gossipy old woman thought it her duty to inform Mother that I was making myself "the talk of the town"—the town of course standing for the English and American colony. Never was I to be seen but in one person's company. More, the pair of us had actually been caught sitting on a seat deep in the woods. Mother's feathers rose at once in defence of her offspring; none the less she was extremely put out, and at the same time not a little embarrassed at having to tackle me on the subject. To her credit be it said that she did so rather half-heartedly, merely asking if I thought it fair to abuse the liberty she had made a point of allowing us. At my age I ought to know where to draw the line, and she expected me to behave more sensibly in future. With so many other acquaintances to choose from, why must it *always* be just this one young man?

At any time intolerant of interference, and enraged by it on the part of an outsider, I tossed my head and refused to be drawn. All Mother got from me was that things were coming to a pretty pass if I had to ask leave before I made a friend. Privately, however, seeing that something must be done, I smuggled an urgent note to my fellow-culprit, begging him to come round that evening, when the rest of the family would be out. This he did, and I told him plainly what had happened. Manlike, he took it more seriously than I; and, for the first time throwing off all constraint, we had an open discussion of our difficulties. By the light of a kitchen lamp—the only one I could lay hands on in my flurry—the glare from whose reflector made what had to be said doubly embarrassing.

The reason for all the pother, the doubts and hesitations, was that we were each of us in a similar quandary. Here was I, who had been brought to Leipzig at what, for Mother, represented a considerable outlay; on whose behalf she put up with living abroad, which she detested, among people she didn't like and whose language she could not master. Yet all this she was willing to endure, provided she might take me back to Australia a finished pianist, there to make not only money but a name for myself. For me now to blurt out that I didn't propose to put my training to any use, but, instead, contemplated marrying an insignificant young man, would be a cruel blow to her dreams and ambitions.

N. was in still worse case. Brought up by his father to be a scientist, he had gone as far as to take his B.Sc., then done what the Germans call *umsatteln*, that is, changed saddles and thrown over science for literature. The inclination had long been working in him, stirred up, to begin with, by Jebb's lectures on the Greek poets, and brought to a head by readings in Carlyle and Goethe. His family, though dismayed, had not opposed him. As, according to him, they would have been quite justified in doing. For

129

they were only moderately well-off, and had a second son on their hands. They also foresaw that openings in literature—and German literature at that—would be few and far between. Had he stuck to science, he might by now have been in a position to support himself. Instead of still having to look to them for his expenses. Altogether, he stood deep in their debt; and to add to it by springing the news of a reckless engagement upon them was not to be thought of.

Or at least not in the meantime—so much I granted. But did they need to know of it, yet awhile? Why not wait to break it to them till he had taken his degree? That would surely make a difference. Thus I argued, trying to be tender of his scruples, even if I didn't understand them. For the idea that one could owe a debt to one's *parents* had never entered my head. I myself had grown up careless and thankless, accepting everything that was done for me as a matter of course, even as my right. And I still think this the healthier attitude. Young shoulders are not built to carry obligations. Least of all to those answerable for their existence.

And, gradually, I got the better of N.'s pride—his "black Scotch pride". For he was, it turned out, just as unwilling as I to let go. Mother would naturally have to be told, but I undertook to manage her.—And I did. We had the stormy scene that may be imagined when she heard of the rout of her cherished plans on my behalf. And all for what? Merely to tie myself up to an impecunious young student, still a year and a half off his degree, and with as good as no prospects. Why, it might be years before he was in a position to marry. To her the whole thing seemed absurd, and the poorest possible ending for the daughter on whom she had pinned so many hopes.—But, as always if she and I really came to grips with each other, she met a will as tough as her own. And when she saw that nothing she could say would move me, that I was bent on what she called ruining my life, she gave in; and yet once more, poor Mother, prepared "to make the best of things".

The first problem was what to do with me in the interim. Apparently it did not occur to anyone to suggest that I worked on and took my certificate, so as to be qualified to add to our resources should the need arise. But in those days wives did not work. The husband alone was expected to provide the wherewithal, and thought relatively little of if he couldn't. And it suited me. For all I could have done was to teach; and, for that, my aptitude was as small as my liking.

However, since fees at the Conservatorium were payable in advance and mine had been settled to the end of the year, it was finally agreed to let me stay till then. And to this decision I owe some of my happiest memories of Leipzig. For though our engagement was not open property, N. and I were allowed a good deal of freedom; Mother assenting, nobody else had the right to interfere. Gossipmongers who ran to her with tales were cut short by the announcement: "they are going to be married".

And we put the time to good use. Before me lies an old notebook, in which I kept a record of all we saw and heard together that winter. The list is a long one, for three or four nights every week found us at the theatre. And it was not to be wondered at, when one looks back on the rich and varied fare the German theatres of that date

131

provided. Operas ranging from Flotow to Wagner, plays as far apart as Dumas and Ibsen—there was little, either old or new, that we didn't get a chance of sampling. We were also lucky enough to come in for some guest-performances by the *Meininger*, then at the height of their fame.

I say nothing of concerts, for, with the exception of the weekly *Gewandhaus* rehearsal, I now seldom went to one. My craze for running after notorieties had fizzled out. Partly because, like any newly-engaged girl, I followed my companion's lead. Besides that, I was at last beginning to sense where my own true inclinations lay—or, rather, where they did not lie. And the meticulous work I put in at the piano interested me less and less.

Over all this, the months raced past, and the day came when I had to face my teachers with the news that I did not intend to complete my course. They took it very differently. Little Schreck at once asked why, and, on being told, gently shook his head, but made no comment. In his eyes, though, I caught a look such as I myself have since given a girl, on hearing that she planned to throw up a promising career for marriage. His said as plainly as words: are they then *all* the same? Has none of them at heart any real aim but to marry? None the grip, the staying-power, the aspiration even, to devote herself to an abstract subject, something not made of flesh and blood—to anything in short *but* a man?

Weidenbach, who always took it as a personal insult did a pupil walk out on him, naturally lost his temper. He thumped the table and shouted, and wouldn't listen when I tried to explain. His point was, that to break off at this juncture was grossly unfair to *him*, after all the work he had put in on me. I had no business to do him out of the decisive year, when he might expect to reap the fruit of his labour. As a rule, his violence could be trusted to get me down, but on this occasion I managed to stand up to him. Stiffened by his reference to the missing year. For the one just past had brought me two experiences that I had no wish to repeat.—That, indeed, I rejoiced to know were behind me, I hoped for ever.

Like any pupil who reached a certain level, I too had been required to show my paces, by performing at a couple of the bi-weekly concerts held in our own concert-hall. And though to all appearances I came through the ordeal tolerably well, what it cost me inwardly nobody but myself knew. It wasn't alone having to face an audience consisting mainly of one's fellow-students, most censorious of critics, nor yet the novice's natural fear of tripping or blundering. No, what did for me, and utterly, were the eyes, the thousands of eyes, all fixed like gimlets on my miserable self, stuck up aloft before them and their helpless prey. The whole time my fingers automatically carried on, I could think only of getting out of range of these eyes, somewhere, anywhere, where they couldn't follow me. It was thus I first became aware of a kink, a mental twist in my nature, that was to prove a lifelong disadvantage. For the aversion to being stared at settled into a definite idiosyncrasy, which I never succeeded in conquering.—And as one cannot be a concert-player without presenting oneself to the public gaze, and such was the fond idea with which I had been brought to Leipzig, there was some reason for reckoning myself a failure all round.

It was just as well, though, I had one thing to be glad of, when the time came to part from the dear old town and its countless associations. For the break proved a great deal harder than I had expected. I felt as if I were being torn in two, leaving the live half of me behind. Rebelliously I listened to the miles roll by, each of which carried me further and further away. How different from the merry party of girls who travelled with us. They were one and all jubilant at the prospect of being back in England.—What had England to offer me?

III

Our homeless state on arriving did not better things. For
months we drifted about, exchanging lodgings in Hampstead for a house in Brixton, loaned Mother by a friend,
thence to Northamptonshire, where the *air* at least was
stimulating, and subsequently to Cambridge where it definitely was not. Here we settled down, and its effect on
me soon made itself felt. I lost all my energy and grew so
thin and pale that a doctor was called in, who dosed me
with tonics. Mother tried to reanimate me by the gift of a
brand-new Bechstein. But I made little use of it. My one real
interest was in the post, with its news of Leipzig and of all
that was going on there—all I was missing. Not to mention
the books that from time to time accompanied the letters.
Without these I should have starved. For in our ignorance
we had rented a house just outside the town boundary, and
the Public Library was closed to us.

I must have been a very trying person to live with—cross-grained and unsociable, for ever slinking off on solitary walks, leaving what gaieties there were to my more adaptable sister. The truth was I felt as much of a misfit here as I had ever done—even in Australia. Indeed there were moments when I could imagine myself back there, all the rich Leipzig years wiped out. An invitation to tea, for example, invariably included the request to "bring your music". Bring my music! What?—a Bach fugue or a sonata by Beethoven? I was so scathing at my would-be-hosts' expense that it led to ructions with Mother.

Then again the few students we chanced to meet seemed strangely immature, mere boys compared with the men we'd known abroad. And as boys they had evidently to be treated. Early on I put my foot in it by lending one some books, amongst others *The Martyrdom of Man*. For this I was taken severely to task by a friend of his, who accused me of trying to "unsettle" him, when I knew that he was destined for the Church.

I was scandalised, and in more ways than one. However I bit my lips and left what I thought unsaid.

And then one day when I was feeling particularly low, there came a letter that abruptly switched my thoughts off myself. The writer was one of our old shipmates on the *Ormuz*, since then but seldom heard from, and, for me, she could not have chosen a luckier moment to break silence. For she wrote to ask if I would care to contribute to a Manuscript Magazine which she and some friends were thinking of starting. Why not, thought I, it might be rather fun, and would at least give me something to do.

And so, though I hadn't tried my hand at writing since leaving Melbourne, I set to and hammered out a piece called *Christmas in Australia*. I took Lamb for my model, whose essays I'd worked through at school, and did my best to imitate him. This was approved, pronounced "very nice, very nice indeed", and it was hoped I would be a regular contributor.

My next effort on the other hand brought me no such encomiums. And I don't wonder. For it had been written solely to please myself, without a thought for the tastes or capacity of my readers. The subject was Ibsen's *Master Builder*, then only just beginning to be heard of in England, and derided as the product of an old man's dotage by most critics. Their dullness exasperated me, and I here set forth, at considerable length, my own opinion of the play and what I believed Ibsen to have meant by it. Neither of which could have mattered a straw to those I wrote for.

Far from being warned by their chilly response—I can only suppose that to feel my pen come alive again unbalanced me—I went on to a still wilder experiment. I now proposed to subject them, chapter by chapter, to the translation of a foreign novel. This book, J. P. Jacobsen's *Niels Lyhne*, one of those sent by N., had stirred me as few books have ever done, either before or since, and I was green enough to imagine that others would be equally impressed.

However they were spared having to struggle through more than a couple of chapters. On his return from Germany N. came down to see us, and when I laid my plan before him he wouldn't hear of it. For he found what I was doing "good—much too good for an amateur magazine". (Amateurs and amateurishness were all his life red rags to him.) He now suggested that I should set to work on the translation in earnest, not in play, and when it was finished we would try and find a publisher for it. To the best of his knowledge the book hadn't yet appeared in English, though out in several other languages—I myself was using the excellent German version. He would write to his Leipzig bookseller for a copy of the original; and, with my knowledge of German and a reliable dictionary to hand, I shouldn't have much difficulty with Danish.

I didn't share his confidence, and the mere thought of a publisher turned me cold. Perhaps, too, the very seductiveness of the proposal weighed against it. To be free to devote myself, day in, day out, to this dear book, and to hear what I did called serious work—the whole thing seemed too good to be true. However in the end N.'s quiet insistence prevailed. Under his lead I began to revise the early chapters, and from then on the Magazine knew me no more.

In the poky little bedroom where Lil and I housed, all I had to write on was the top of a marble wash-stand. But when not long after we moved to London, or more precisely Balham, to share an over-large house with some Australian friends, things were different. Here I had a big room and to myself, and was in nobody's way. Moreover being three floors up, it was well above backyards and dustbins, and overlooked the remains of what must once have been a park. Several magnificent old trees were still standing, and of an evening I could watch the sun go down behind them.

Here I was tolerably content. Our housemates were not of the interfering kind; they let me be, which was all I asked of them or of anybody. For my work on *Niels* continued to absorb me, and I felt that at last I had discovered what I liked best to do. To sit alone and unobserved, behind a shut door, and play with words and ponder phrases. (What a contrast to the odious publicity of the concert-platform! How I could ever have imagined myself fitted for it I didn't know.)

And this conviction steadily gaining ground, I walked Mother off to Tottenham Court Road, there to buy, at secondhand and out of my puny dress-allowance, a "real" writing-table. The one I chose cost only a little over three pounds, but it was well-made and not unsightly, and had certainly been built to last. For the next ten years it went everywhere with me, journeying to and fro on the continent and eventually landing back in England. Both *Maurice Guest* and *The Getting of Wisdom* were written at it. Only when I came to the *Trilogy* did it prove too small for all the maps and reference-books that were necessary. But I could not bring myself to part with so old a friend. And to-day it still occupies a place in a back bedroom.

To revert to Balham. Though life there ran more smoothly for me, really happy I wasn't and couldn't be while N. and I were apart, meeting only at wide intervals. As for our marriage, it seemed as remote as ever. For though he had returned from Leipzig with a first-class degree, he could find no employment. The universities one and all adhered to the hoary standpoint that none but Germans were capable of lecturing on German literature. He applied in turn, and in vain, for posts falling vacant at St. Andrews, Edinburgh, Manchester and even Glasgow; everywhere alike he had to see a foreigner preferred. One of these places, and one which in after years was to invest him with an Hon. D. Litt., dealing him so rude a snub that even he, the least resentful of mortals, never forgot it.

Meanwhile he sat at home, where things were the reverse of easy for him. Not that he was openly reproached for the plight in which he had landed himself; but to one of his temperament, the chill silence, the pinched lips and averted eyes that accompanied his successive failures cut just as deep. To get away from them, he went out and taught for six months at a girls' school. After that he tried his hand at journalism. Finally, on the advice of a friend who had some influence with a publisher, he set to editing a couple of German texts. This was more in his own line, and he got a certain satisfaction out of it.

I was glad because it brought him to London, to the British Museum. He naturally stayed with us, and I seized every chance to fight the depressing effects of his home. In all sincerity. For where N. was concerned I never lost confidence, never doubted that, given time, he would make good, and everything come right for us.

At the moment I had a personal reason to feel hopeful. *Niels*, finished and copied out—in a hand that bore no resemblance to my youthful scrawl—had been offered to a firm that made a side-line of foreign novels and found worth publishing. When it appeared I was to get forty pounds for it. This represented an enormous sum to me, and I could not but take a rosy view of the future. N. was gratified to hear his own judgment confirmed, pleased to see me in good spirits, and himself returned to Scotland in a rather cheerier frame of mind.

It was short-lived, for I had soon to report a fresh upset at our end. The lease of the Balham house was on the point of expiring, and, instead of renewing it, our fellow-occupants contemplated going home, to Australia. If they did we should have to turn out, squeeze ourselves anew into some poky villa—a prospect none of us relished. Mother too was unsettled by hearing so much talk about the homeland. She still sighed for it, and for the many relatives and friends she had left. The sole thing that kept her hanging on in England was my uncertain future. She must first know what was to become of me.

Here however Lil put in her spoke, by suggesting that we should go abroad again. Unlike me she had not lost interest in music; on the contrary had pegged away at her violin wherever we were, with the best master available. This was all very well; what she needed, said she, was to hear more music, and to be amongst fellow-students. Germany was not so far off that I couldn't come back to get married, if N. *should* happen to drop into a post. Mother dilly-dallied for a while, but her own love of change was as strong as ever, and Lil's needs offered an excuse for seeing a fresh bit of the world. Besides, why should *I* always be the only person to be considered?—And so once more we found ourselves on the move.

The same restless blood ran in my veins, nor can I honestly say I was sorry to get out of a London suburb. But to N. our desertion seemed the last straw. Afterwards, he admitted to having wondered if he would ever see me again. Finding herself so far south, Mother might yield to one of her incalculable impulses and carry us both off home. For

141

this time Munich was our destination, and, once there, we would be within reach of either Naples or Brindisi. Had I suspected the existence of such a bogey I should have made short work of it. For in going back to Germany I had a scheme of my own, which for certain reasons I preferred to say nothing about till I got there.

Just what took us to Munich is no longer clear. Anyhow, since I had to be parted from N., it was all the same to me where we went; and I could not foresee how lucky this rather random choice would prove. At first I regretted it, for, unlike old Leipzig, Munich wasn't an easy place to feel at home in. It was too big and sprawly, and, besides that, it catered for so many conflicting interests. Of these, painting and painters were shown most consideration, music coming off a rather shabby second-best. The teaching at the Academy, for one thing, seemed incredibly superficial compared with that of the Con. And so it was with much else besides. Not even the world-famed opera under Possart came up to my expectations. For the *Hoftheater* was so vast that few voices could fill it without a strain. Our own beloved Moran-Olden, whom we here met once more, was a case in point. In Leipzig we had hung on her lips; now she too sounded harsh and shrill.—Altogether, on first acquaintance, Munich had only two genuine attractions. The radiant blue of its skies, set off by compact white masses of cloud that might have been hewn in marble; and the snow-fed, galloping Isar, after the fetid Pleisse and the muddy Cam.

The climate was also a disappointment. By coming further south we had innocently looked for warmth, and, instead, found ourselves perched on a plateau, within sight of snow-mountains and reach of their icy winds. We didn't improve things by taking a flat that faced north and got no sun. Mother and I, who spent the greater part of the day indoors, were the sufferers. I was never free of a cold or a cough, she had to contend with mysterious aches and pains.—Incidentally, this was the first climate Mother had failed to stand up to; and, had we only had eyes to see, a thought to spare from ourselves, we might have taken warning.

But we had come to believe her health unshakeable, and at present were both more than ever engrossed in our own concerns. Lil, elated at finding herself accepted as a pupil by Benno Walther, the then-time leader of the orchestra, and with numerous friends of the sort she'd wanted, naturally paid little attention to what went on at home. I was equally sunk in my self-imposed job of teaching English, to a group of university-students; and between-whiles in concocting reports on the opera for the home papers.—These last I may say didn't get me far. The music journals were quite willing to take them, but wouldn't or couldn't pay; the rest ignored them. With the exception of one big Northern Daily, whose editor, though he omitted to print what I sent, wrote me a personal letter commending its neat and unobtrusive style.

But money was at that time more important to me than praise. For I was out to prove to N. that I could earn enough to keep myself, and would not fall a burden on him. In the event, that was, of his yielding to my persuasions and listening to my private plan. What I wanted him to do was to give up the futile struggle, acknowledge himself beaten, turn his back on home and home prejudices, and follow us out to Germany. For I had become convinced that he was chasing a shadow, waiting on a preferment that would never materialise, or would always pass to another.

The idea that he and I should join forces and fend for ourselves was not exactly new. As long ago as Leipzig we had faced such a contingency. Then however only half seriously. Now I came back on it in earnest, reinforced by all N. had gone through in the interval, and by my own recent experiences. For money was of course the chief consideration, money and how to make it; and here I could reassure him. If a nobody like myself could get pupils, for him with his degrees it would be easier still. He'd probably find himself snowed under, able to pick and choose, and to ask a tidy price for his lessons.—And from this point on to the various others that had to be driven home, each of them argued to the best of my ability. I didn't make much of a success of it; the time-gaps between letters seemed to destroy their connectedness, and N., who thought the whole thing rank nonsense, had a way of letting my arguments pass without comment. In fact the only concession I ever drew from him was that the articles on German literature, which he was beginning to get inserted in monthlies and quarterlies, might perhaps carry more weight if they came from Germany.

Some effect my letters may have had all the same. For in the course of that summer, and entirely on his own initiative, he wrote to several professors of English at German universities, inquiring if any of them happened to need an English lector. Unfortunately nobody did; but one and all took the trouble to reply respectfully. This seemed to me

144

a good omen, after the scant courtesy with which his own country treated him, and it helped to strengthen my hope of ultimately winning him round.

But here if Mother didn't come out with an idea of her own, and one so different that at first it threatened to spoil everything. Not for me; I leapt at it, having no pride where she was concerned. But N. couldn't be expected to feel as I did.

Her proposal—made with her usual directness, not to say bluntness—was that he and I should just take the three hundred pounds laid by for our wedding-present, and "get married and be done with it!" She was sick and tired, she declared, of seeing me so moody and unsettled, frittering my time away over things I didn't care twopence about. Marriage would alter all that; and our two brains put together could be trusted to make good.

More she declined to say; and I often puzzled over her real motives for this bold and, in a way, so un-motherly a step, considering the various risks that we ran. What had prompted it only became clear when she lay sick of her last illness.

My immediate problem was N., who needed to be more or less battered into compliance. In after years I used laughingly to tell him that never, before or since, had I worked so hard as at that time. How I overcame his scruples is my own affair. I managed it, bit by bit, though right up to the end I did not feel absolutely sure of him.

We first thought of being married in Munich. But I soon saw that it wasn't going to be easy. The number of papers to be filled in, the certificates and proofs of identity required before the Germans permitted us to marry! *My* papers, even suppose them to exist, would take months to get hold of. We were still undecided what it was best to do, when an Australian-Irish friend of Mother's wrote warmly inviting us to have the wedding from her house in Dublin. This of course would be a solution, and Mother was all in favour of it. But of old I had suffered under our hostess's rather lavish hospitality, her love for a festive gathering; and both N. and I would have preferred just to creep into a Registrar's office.

With such a "hole-and-corner proceeding" Mother refused to have anything to do, and so to Ireland she and I went, where I put in the necessary weeks while the banns were called. And where I first got to know my father's birthplace, and the home of his ancestors. Unfortunately it was a bad time of year, mid-winter; the clouds remained unbroken, a perpetual soft rain fell. Christmas, too, was at the door; and, search my memory as I will, my only recollections of Dublin are of mud and drunkenness.

I walked the dirty streets, with thoughts far removed. For now that it seemed as if the end was actually at hand I was haunted by a fear lest some accident should befall N. at the eleventh hour. The night he crossed I sat at the window listening to the splash-dash of an excited sea, that might even yet swallow him up.

However none of my heated imaginings took shape, the boat neither went down, nor was he washed overboard; and, in due course, he and the friend who had come with him presented themselves at Clontarf parish church. Nor did any member of the congregation rise to show cause or just impediment. We were married, safely and soundly married, and the last of my grisly forebodings joined their forebears.

The sole contretemps, if such it can be called, reserved itself for the Breakfast; and I for one knew nothing of it till long afterwards.

It seems that one of the family, entering the dining-room for a final glance at the arrangements, was aghast to see that we should be thirteen at table. To the superstitious Irish this denoted luck of the worst kind to some members of the party and she did her utmost to render it void. Without a word to anybody an extra chair was squeezed in, and a semi-invalid sister brought from her couch to occupy it. But it was too late, the ban had already worked; and of those present sure enough two died before the prescribed year was out. The husband of a cousin of mine, and Mother.

"From Ireland N. and I made our way back to Munich along the Rhine which I had never seen…"

This fragment constitutes the last effort Henry Handel Richardson made to continue the story of her youth. At this point the pencil literally fell from her fingers, which had become too weak to hold it. To me falls the task of stating the facts of the seven years which followed her marriage on December 30th, 1895, to bring *Myself When Young* up to the point where she had meant to leave it—that is, to the end of her sojourn in Germany and the beginning of their life in England in 1903. In doing so I am drawing partly on some notes made by Professor Robertson for his own use—he intended, had he outlived Henry Handel, himself to write something about their early years together—and partly on what H.H.R. has told me of these days. She herself left no notes or indication as to how she meant to proceed, and it was quite by chance that I found her husband's scribbled and almost indecipherable jottings.

After a brief visit to J. G. R.'s parents in Glasgow, the newly-married pair travelled to Munich, passing through Bonn and other Rhine towns. There they made their home in a tiny three-roomed flat, Thorwaldsenstrasse 33, in the Nymphenburg district of the city—that is, the working-class quarter. This was in January, 1896. They had no financial resources other than the three hundred pounds given them by Mrs Richardson as a wedding-present, and this greatly worried J. G. R.'s careful Scottish soul. But, characteristically, H. H. R.'s view was: "We will live on that as long as we can; and, if nothing else turns up, we will at least have had some happiness *together*."

She proved the wiser, for, as he liked to say in after years, from the moment he put himself in her hands, his luck began to turn. And to the end of his life he always trusted her judgment, even when the things she wanted to do seemed to his cautious mind reckless to the point of folly.

J. G. R. was immediately invited to contribute a bi-annual article on German literature to a new German review, *Cosmopolis*, and by the end of January the publisher of H. H. R.'s excellent translation of Jacobsen's *Niels Lyhne* wrote asking her to undertake further translations from the Danish. Of these the only one she completed was *The Fisher Lass* by Björnson. She would have liked to translate a work by Brandes, but the speed at which the publisher required this to be done made it an impossible task for her.

Their life was full and happy, for, besides their work, they frequently occupied gallery seats at the theatre, and as H.H.'s mother and sister also lived in Munich there were many social gatherings and a "quartet" which met and played regularly.

In letters to his father and mother during the first four months at Munich J.G.R. speaks of many purchases made for their little home; and on April 28th he writes: "I miss the garden; we have to be content with pot plants and cut flowers. Ett has quite a small garden in this way now; the plants make our windows look very nice." And later in the same letter: "We have been just counting up that we are sixteen weeks married—time flies! But what *very* happy weeks they have been!"

That first Easter they visited Starnberg, where the snow was still on the ground, and on May 7th came the invitation to J.G.R. to become a lecturer in the University of Strassburg. This, though the salary was very small, at least gave some surety for the future.

That summer H.H. and her husband made, in the shape of a walking-tour, the journey from Munich to Strassburg, to inspect the latter place and find a house. They went by way of the Bavarian Highlands to Innsbruck; thence up the Arlberg and over the mountains to Bregenz; by boat to Lindau and Constance, and from there by train through the Black Forest to Strassburg, arriving home again on August 6th.

On September 25th, 1896, the doors of the little flat—to which they always applied the words of Elisabeth in Liszt's oratorio of that name: "Wie ist dies Haus voll Sonnenschein!"—were finally closed.

Their new house was at No. 6, Sternwartstrasse, and to it their few goods and chattels were moved at the end of September. To quote J. G. R.: "The Sternwartstrasse house was soon made homelike—Henry having a genius for doing things on small means." At first they were unfavourably impressed by Strassburg as compared with Munich. The Black Forest and the Vosges seemed tame after the wild Bavarian country. But they found friends among the circle of young university teachers, and the charm of excursions into the Black Forest was soon discovered.

With their improved finances, H. H. felt she could afford to keep a maid. Their mother having done everything for the two girls throughout their lives, when H. H. married she was completely inexperienced in all domestic matters. A few extracts from her letters to her mother at this time give some impression of her first household experiments:—

"October 6th, 1896. ...If houses are cheaper than in Munich, all eatables are dearer. This is owing to the blessed octroi, a tax that is laid on everything that comes inside the town walls. Fancy we had not been in the house half an hour before an octroi official arrived to know what we had brought with us in the way of spirits, Brenn-materialien, new furniture, etc. He took a note of our two bottles of Spiritus and Petroleum...

The people downstairs are very decent and tell us where the cheapest things are to be had. The dialect is terrible; I wish you could hear our milkman..."

"October 13th, 1896... Many thanks for your long letter of Sunday. It was very good of you to sit down and write so much, and it will be a great help to me. I shall keep it as a kind of Cookery Book in Petto.

I feel quite a lady at large this morning, having someone else to do the house for me. The last two weeks have been hard work for us both. I hope things will go all right.

It's too soon of course to say how they *will* go—she only arrived yesterday afternoon. I don't know whether I like her or not yet, which is perhaps rather a good sign, for I always end by disliking the people I take a fancy to at first. I would prefer to find out her qualities like her faults by degrees. She wears a fringe and several rings, but so far she has worked well, and seems obliging. She had the kitchen table as white as snow before she had been long here.

This morning she has virtually done the house out and it is not quite ten. We have yet to see how the cooking goes...

By the way the female downstairs performs the Sultan's Polka, and not as well as you do. Thank goodness she doesn't play more than about half an hour a day.

The butcher has just sent the bones—I wish you saw them—they would all go into a cup. I ordered for 30 pf.; how many do you get for that? In England I know it was twice as much. On Sunday however with the veal he sent a foot, and though I didn't know its properties I soon discovered them from the jelly it made. That gave us soup yesterday—with sago in it—and if it is good there was enough left for to-day. I would give something though to have you to apply to, to know if it is good and what to do with it! I can't *tret* firmly *auf* in the kitchen at all, being too conscious of my ignorance..."

"Wed. afternoon [October 1896]... Thanks for all the cookery items. We are getting on all right, although the apple-pudding to-day was a failure. When I turned the basin upside down for five minutes as you said, all the apples came out! Finally we had to take it out of the basin altogether, so you can imagine it was rather funny.

The oven went badly to-day; it takes fits and we don't understand it well yet. The fire burns and everything boils, but nothing will bake in the oven and it is so small.

I am very well satisfied with Mathilde, and would like to leave the cooking to her altogether. She is an excellent worker, and quick at picking up cooking. If only you were here to show her. Couldn't you run through for a couple of weeks?

On my neck at present, asleep, is—a cat. Yes we have got a little fellow and he has made the smudges on this letter. We advertised yesterday, and one turned up at four this afternoon. He is very like Turvy, almost the same colours, and the boy said he was four months old, but he looks younger. His name is Monkey [Punkah]. He is very lively and playful, and I am keeping a sharp eye on him!

We have not had any further visitors. G. has almost got through his list. On Sunday we are to go to tea with K. ...at five o'clock. The little man is showing himself very kind and friendly..."

"Tuesday, October 27th, 1896... The great event of this week was the arrival of a piano. One wet day we suddenly decided that we couldn't do without one any longer. It is of course an upright—the room couldn't hold a grand—but it's a very good one. Costs 15 mks a month. It is delightful to have it and I have been waking the house up a little, for the Frl. downstairs performs the Sultan's Polka and up above they don't even get that length. The Herr and Frau Rechnungsrat were full of the "wunderschöne Musik". I shouldn't say this was a musical place, although there's a Con.

Our little gas stove came yesterday, but the meter is not here yet. It has just two burners for kettles and Töpfe; doesn't roast or bake of course. It will be cheaper than Spiritus.

I am gradually finding out shops. Have got a grocer not very far from here where Petrol. only costs 20 pf. Butter is 68 the half just now and eggs 8 each. But I get quite a good sugar for 28 a lb..."

In November Henry Handel's mother died, from peritonitis following on the appendicitis for which at that time no operation was considered feasible. This event had a profound effect on H. H., and ultimately led to the rather bitter short story, first published in the *English Review* (1911) under the title *Death*. This was subsequently re-named *Mary Christina*, and appeared in her *Two Studies* (1931) and *The End of a Childhood* (1934). In later life she told me her views on death had greatly changed, but that to see her strong, robust mother—who had fought through such a chequered life with undaunted courage and resource—have to die at the age of 57 in such a slow, agonising manner had shattered and angered her.

I found among H.H.'s papers an unfinished "diary" account of her mother's illness. This foreshadows the vividness and power with which she was later to portray the deaths of John Turnham, Richard Mahony and Daniel Liszt, together with the effect of these tragedies on those who had to watch them.

Mrs Richardson's death, however, had the result of easing the young couple's financial anxieties still further. During 1896 their combined literary earnings had not been very much above £100.

The year 1897 was a momentous one in H.H.R.'s life as a writer. In the spring of that year she wrote a centenary article on Schubert, which appeared in the *Speaker* (Jan. 30th), as also did "Ibsen in Translation" (July 10th), in which she made a slashing attack on William Archer's translation of *John Gabriel Borkman*. This stung Archer into writing a long letter of self-defence in the same periodical on July 24th. Henry Handel also wrote an article on "German Women Writers", which was not published; and on July 20th a critical study of Jacobsen was finished and sent to *Cosmopolis*, where it appeared in November, 1897.

To those who know H.H.R.'s subsequent literary achievements the most interesting date in these years is September 27th, 1897. On this there appears in her sparse diary the one-word entry: "novel". The thought of original writing must have occurred to her before, but it was about this time that the first tentative beginnings were made to *Maurice Guest*, although the completion and publication of the book did not take place until eleven years later. To quote from J. G. R.'s jottings: "Possibly the first suggestion of such creative writing had come to her from her husband, namely that she should utilise her own Leipzig experiences to form a novel of a musician who failed to make good. Progress was exceedingly slow and tentative at first; but from now on the word 'novel' or 'work' or a pet name for her new venture, 'Tinkling Cymbals', appears frequently in the diary. I still remember the day she suddenly told me modestly that her people had begun to speak of their own accord—this having been one of the great initial difficulties. By February 4th, 1898, evidently some progress had been made as we find the entry: 'N. read *Tinkling Cymbals* to me.'"

That spring a tour was made in Italy, and in summer H. H. won the ladies' tennis championship at Strassburg. In this year, too, the pair acquired bicycles and made many excursions on them. In August a party walking-tour in Switzerland took them over much ground, including the Grimsel, Furka and Gotthard passes. In October they bicycled to Karlsruhe to hear, at the *Hoftheater*, on two successive evenings, Berlioz' *Trojanes*. H. H. once described to me how, on the return journey, her back tyre collapsed; and how, because of this, they had had to make a wild dash over cobbled streets, she riding on the flat tyre, in order to catch a train by which they could get back to Strassburg before J. G. R.'s free time expired.

There is little mention of "work" in the 1898 diary, but one entry states that H. H. took French lessons.

Towards the end of December, 1898, Henry Handel had a very serious illness. Awakening one night to find that she could not breathe, she struggled first to her knees, then to her feet, in a desperate effort to get air to her lungs. This was the beginning of acute bronchitis, with which she fought until the end of January, when, as her doctor feared a grave lung affection, she was sent to Bordighera to recuperate. J. G. R. was almost desperate with worry during her illness, especially as he had often to leave her in the house alone while he gave his lectures at the University.

Her departure for the Riviera was their first separation; he had to stay and continue his work. With H. H. went the "Mat" (Miss Main) of the Norwegian holiday described in *Myself When Young*. During the weeks that followed the word "worked" appears occasionally in her diary, together with notes of much very miscellaneous reading.

On March 2nd, 1899, J. G. R. travelled to Bordighera to join her, and now occurred a minor tragedy which neither of them ever forgot. H. H.'s illness and her enforced stay on the Riviera were naturally very costly, and J. G. R.'s father sent him £40 to help meet the expense. One day, while they were sitting in the woods, he placed the wallet containing this money on the seat beside him, and when they rose and walked away he left it lying there. They never saw it again.

On the way back to Strassburg they spent two weeks in Lugano, arriving home on April 18th. The Riviera had not had the hoped-for effect on H. H.'s health—it was too dusty for a hyper-sensitive throat and the change from sun to shade temperature was too violent. What really cured and set her up was a long holiday that summer, spent at Badenweiler, in the pine-laden air of the Black Forest. She sturdily maintained that it was her throat which had not stood the constant bronchitic cough, and that her lungs had never been affected. Be this as it may, the illness certainly left her throat permanently weak.

In Strassburg was formed H. H.'s habit of always keeping a cat beside her as a pet—a habit she retained for the rest of her life. Though she was very fond of dogs, she said that cats fascinated her; they were so completely self-sufficient and independent, and she felt honoured when they bestowed their affection on her. During the Strassburg years she had two of these pets in succession: "Punkah" ("Polly-cat") and "Jigger". To the first-named she wrote the words and music of some quaint little songs she called the "Punkah-Lieder".

Of interest during 1899 are short entries in the diary, such as "Lil read chapters IV and V". And two which have a bearing on the little Strassburg story, *The Life and Death of Peterle Lüthy*; June 3rd: "went to see E.'s baby"; June 25th: "went to see dead baby".

In this year there was some excitement over the engagement of her sister to a Munich eye-specialist: Dr. Otto Neustatter. On December 21st the engagement was celebrated in Strassburg. The wedding took place on April 5th, 1900; and on the 10th the Robertsons moved into a new house: Twingerstrasse 5.

In 1900 J. G. R. was busily engaged in writing his *History of German Literature*. This was accepted for publication by Messrs. William Blackwood of Edinburgh, and towards the end of the year "proofs began to come, in the reading of which Henry was of great help to me". At this period J. G. R. also did much reviewing of German books for *The Times*. He was offered a professorship at Ann Arbor, but does not state his reasons for refusing the post. The summer was spent with his parents in Wigtownshire.

On November 5th there was a little tragedy in the death of the beloved cat "Punkah". H.H. always took the death of her animals very hardly; they meant as much to her as people, and she frequently bemoaned the fact that their lives were so short.

By 1901 the Robertsons had a pleasant circle of friends in Strassburg, and made many delightful excursions to the Black Forest and the Vosges. In June they visited Munich, and that summer was spent in the Bavarian Highlands, at the small village of Marquartstein, "under somewhat primitive conditions."

During this year H.H. took Italian lessons; she also noted in her diary: "Resolved to note what I am working at and to read English." In accordance with this the progress of *Maurice* is more exactly noted.

"Jan. 1st: 'Schilsky Schlussscene'."
"Jan. 6th: 'Beginning of Chapter IX in second form'."
"Jan. 10th: 'Rose paragraph'."
"Jan. 14th: 'Chapter IV, scene between Krafft, Madeleine and Maurice'."
"Jan. 16th: 'Close of Chapter IV'."
"Jan. 28th: 'Chapter VII, Anfang'."
"Feb. 6th: 'Part 2. Chapters I and II'."
"March 8th: 'Maurice and Louise. End chapters'."

This was evidently a year of pretty steady work on *Maurice*.

H.H.'s diary in 1902 has few entries until Sept. 9th, when she wrote: "No diary kept: because from July 22nd on I was too happy and too *unbewusst* to think about it."

During this year J. G. R. was made Professor at Strassburg and H. H. R. was thenceforth "Frau Professor".

They went to Locarno in April, and again spent the summer in Marquartstein, making a long walking-tour to St. Johann in Tirol. On Sept. 13th they returned to Strassburg and on the same date J.G.R.'s *History of German Literature* was published. This had far-reaching results, for during a visit to his home in Glasgow at the end of December the appointment to the Chair of German Literature in the University of London was suggested to J. G. R. The matter was finally settled in April, 1903, and on the 19th of that month the Robertsons, after selling off their furniture and packing their books, left for London and occupied lodgings at 18, Willow Road, Hampstead.

In June they took a new house which was then being built: 5 Lyon Road, Harrow-on-the-Hill. After this a return was made to Strassburg for a final packing, and the summer was once more spent at Marquartstein.

That autumn J. G. R. went to London alone, living in lodgings in Bloomsbury until the Harrow house was habitable, while Henry Handel remained in Munich to await the birth of "Lil's" son, Walter Lindesay Neustatter, which took place on December 7th, 1903. It was during this period that H. H. R. took the lessons in Harmony and Counterpoint from Ludwig Thuille, referred to in Chapter I, Part II, of *Myself When Young*.

In January, 1904, H.H.R. arrived in her new home at Harrow, accompanied by Fräulein Irene Stumpp, who remained with her as secretary and housekeeper for many years, both there and, from 1910 on, in London—at 90 Regent's Park Road. I now quote J.G.R. once more: "I had a warm welcome for them and a new section of our life opened."

"Thus ended seven happy years of very varied experiences.

"These Strassburg years were fruitful in composition— dozens of charming little songs and even the beginning of a 'symphonic poem' *Der Herbst* (afterwards arranged for violin, viola and voice) which has left its traces in *Maurice*... Often H.H. would say she would rather be able to compose songs than write books. A large part of her musical interest was concentrated on Richard Strauss, then at his zenith. Once she had come in contact with him at Marquartstein.

"These years it is true were much punctuated by frequent illness, and one serious illness. Our excursions were often too strenuous and overtaxed her by no means robust health. But it was perhaps the happiest period of our lives.

"We left Germany unwillingly, missed bitterly the Black Forest and Vosges and our circle of intimate friends in Strassburg. And indeed Henry never reconciled herself to life in England. For years she felt a constant regret and hankering after the Continent; we had hoped with the improved financial conditions to see as much of the old summer haunts (and Strassburg in spring) as before; but the long railway journey made it exhausting, and more difficult. It was not the same. And walking in Middlesex was not walking in the Black Forest. It was also not easy to make new friends like the old; for one thing, settling in Harrow precluded the possibility of doing so in the first seven years when new intimacies might have been formed. And the views of the new friends were not Henry's. Our attempt to introduce the old Sunday afternoon 'at homes' which had been so pleasant a feature of the Twingerstrasse house was something of a failure.

"The house in Lyon Road was pleasant and the garden a source of pleasure. But going into London for theatre or concert was strenuous as the ten minutes' walk to such things in Strassburg had never been. These unsympathetic surroundings and conditions had perhaps one good result: that in Harrow Henry buried herself as never before in her book.

"The ties with Germany were kept alive by summer visits to Bavaria. North Germany we did not see again until we revisited Leipzig—something of a disappointment after the magic halo with which in our memories it was surrounded—in 1907, to verify the *locale* of *Maurice*.

"In the Strassburg years Henry's reading was very wide. [Her lists for 1898 and 1899 number well over a hundred books read in each of these years.] My work for *Cosmopolis* and *The Times* brought into the house the newest German literature, which she followed—the realistic movement—with intense interest. While the Strassburg library provided the opportunity of familiarising herself with the great French literature: Hugo, Stendhal, Flaubert, Balzac, Maupassant, Zola, etc. Also Tolstoi and Dostoievsky. She read each new work of Ibsen and Björnson: a new work by Brandes was an event.

"On all these things our little Strassburg circle could talk, and discussed them with similar interest. Of this there was little or nothing in London; and she felt spiritually isolated. Also she found no congenial friends interested in music. Thus her life became, unfortunately, more solitary, and the 'living alone' only increased with the years."

Here I come to the end of Professor Robertson's "jottings"; and to the finish of the period H. H. R. meant to cover—had she lived to do so. I lay down my pen with a feeling of bitter sorrow that the conclusion of the frank and illuminating story of this great writer's youth has had to be so baldly stated—and by another hand than hers.

OLGA M. RONCORONI
Fairlight, Sussex
February 17th, 1947

Text Classics

A Change in the Lighting
Amy Witting
Introduced by Ashley Hay

Selected Stories
Amy Witting
Introduced by Melanie Joosten

Isobel on the Way to the Corner Shop
Amy Witting
Introduced by Maria Takolander

I Own the Racecourse!
Patricia Wrightson
Introduced by Kate Constable

textclassics.com.au